No-nonsense
VEGETABLE
GARDENING

How to grow vegetables in small gardens

CHRISTINE WALKDEN

SIMON &
SCHUSTER
ILLUSTRATED

London · New York · Sydney · Toronto

A CBS COMPANY

Dedicated to all my friends who love and help me,
and in reality make all I do possible.

SIMON &
SCHUSTER
ILLUSTRATED

First published in Great Britain by Simon & Schuster UK Ltd, 2011 A CBS Company

Text copyright © Christine Walkden Design and new photography copyright © Simon & Schuster UK Ltd

SIMON AND SCHUSTER ILLUSTRATED BOOKS
Simon & Schuster UK, 222 Gray's Inn Road, London WC1X 8HB www.simonandschuster.co.uk

10 9 8 7 6 5 4 3 2 1

Editorial Director Francine Lawrence **Managing Editor** Nicky Hill **Project Editor** Serena Dilnot
Design Jane Humphrey **New Photography** Jacqui Hurst **Picture Researcher** Emma O'Neill **Illustrator** John Erwood
Production Manager Katherine Thornton

Colour reproduction by Dot Gradations Ltd, UK Printed and bound in Singapore
ISBN 978-1-84737-864-4

CONTENTS

If at first you don't succeed, sow again...

Christine

THE NO-NONSENSE APPROACH TO GARDENING

When I was nine years old I sliced off the top of a carrot, put it in a saucer of water and watched it grow. This was my first experience with vegetable growing. I then started to grow mustard and cress on a flannel on my bedroom windowsill and realised how easy it was to turn those specks of dust into a growing and living thing. I was hooked. I obtained a full-sized allotment from the local authority (my mum had to sign for it) and I was away.

The site needed to be cleared of all weeds and brambles and the old allotmenters told me how to do this properly – by digging them out. It was extremely hard work but I did manage it. In the spring the old chaps came and showed me where I was going wrong and then as the plants grew I started reading gardening books. This started me on the path to success. I learned from my mistakes and just kept trying until I got it right. Maybe that's how my no-nonsense approach to gardening was born.

I grew all the normal vegetables that you would expect and then as they matured I sold the surplus to people in the road where I lived and took them to school and sold them to my schoolteachers. I just loved the fact that you could pop some seed into the ground and after a couple of weeks green shoots started to show through. It was so exciting. I got a great thrill out of caring for them and growing them so that they were as good as or better than the ones on the other allotments. Looking back, perhaps I should not have been so competitive, but I was young, and it did make me focus on gardening techniques and learning from books.

I think the most useful lesson I was taught was not to give up if it did not work the first time, but to ask why this was the case. Questions that needed to be asked were: How old was the seed and was it still alive? Was the soil temperature warm enough (or had I sown the seed into soil that was too cold because I was so eager to get started)? Had I sown the seed at the correct depth (too shallow and it would dry out, too deep and I would bury it)? If it had germinated and come through the soil, had it been attacked by pests or diseases? Had I hoed it off when weeding, due to lack of experience and skill in using the hoe? Had it dried out?

Many of these questions were answered through observation and by thinking about what I had done. The way you actually learn to garden is by gardening, and I was learning how to grow all sorts of crops. As each year passes you too will learn so much about growing vegetables. It is this process of accumulating experience and knowledge that keeps me at it even after forty years. I still love growing.

How much space do you need?

If you want to grow vegetables you don't need a large garden or expensive equipment. My own garden is about 53m (175ft) long by 10m (35ft) wide, and the veg patch is 10m (35ft) long and 8m (25ft) wide. It is surrounded by a fence which keeps it sheltered from wind.

The more space you have, the more you can grow, but you do not need a garden to grow vegetables. You can start by growing things in teacups, small pots or seedtrays. These are called micro-greens. Sprouting seeds, cress and mustard will grow in very small spaces and you can harvest a crop of salad leaves several times from a seedtray. There are also smaller varieties of vegetables that will produce successful crops when grown in a 30cm (12in) plant pot.

With a bigger container, such as a window box, you can grow a full selection of salad crops, and a small raised bed can produce a whole range of vegetable crops. With more space and time you can have all the veg a family could want.

chapter 1

GETTING STARTED

GETTING STARTED

To help you get the best out of your garden, look at the following questions. They will direct you to the sections of the book applicable to your garden, and will give you some indication of what you need to do before you start any job.

1. Where will you grow your vegetables? Do you have a suitable site in your garden?
Is your garden very shady or very windy? For information on site selection, see page 12

2. What is your soil like?
To find out what type of soil you have, see page 16

3. Have you ever tested your soil's pH level?
To learn more about how the acidity or alkalinity of your soil will affect your vegetables, see page 17

4. How good is your soil's drainage?
When it rains very heavily, does water tend to run off your soil? Perhaps it sinks in, but the soil stays wet and sticky? Or does the water disappear quickly and the soil dries fast? For information about drainage, see page 18

5. How do you feel about digging?
Is digging something new for you? Perhaps you are thinking about using a rotavator instead? For information on digging, see page 20

6. How can you make the most of a small or medium-sized garden?
For suggestions, see page 26

7. Has your garden ever received manure, compost or fertiliser?
To find out how to make the best use of these materials, see page 36

8. Do you raise your own plants and know what aids are available to you?
If you have never tried to grow your own plants, now is the time to be adventurous. For information on seed and seed sowing, see page 46

9. When should you water your seedlings and plants?
The answers are in chapter 5 – see page 62

10. How do you keep your garden free from weeds?
Chapter 14 has information about preventing and controlling weeds – see page 162

11. Are your plants disfigured, distorted, stunted or ill-looking?
To find out about pests and diseases and what to do in the event of an attack, see page 165

12. Are you making the best use of your contact with other people who grow vegetables and do you know where to get help and advice?
To find out more, see page 169

SITE SELECTION

Aspect

Where should I site my vegetable garden?
Vegetables can be grown in all sorts of positions. However, avoid dense shade, very exposed sites and those which are waterlogged. Ideally, the site should be in an open position with a sunny outlook (or aspect), usually found in a garden that faces south.

The soil in a sunny site will be warmer in the spring. This warmth will aid the germination of those crops sown in the early part of the year. If your plot is in another aspect, you will need to sow your crops a little later in the season, when the soil has warmed up (see page 51). Plants grown in a south-facing garden will also be earlier to mature than those grown in a north-facing plot due to the warmth of the sun warming up the site more quickly.

Avoid a very sloping site if possible, as the soil can be easily eroded. On light or sandy soils, the soil may be washed away by watering if it is on a slope.

Choose a site with the minimum of obstructions from buildings and trees, which can create dense shade.

Vegetable crops do not enjoy shade and it prevents plants achieving their maximum growth. As well as causing shade, overhanging trees compete for food, water and light, and may also provide an over-wintering site for pests and diseases.

What can I do if my garden is very shady?
If light is blocked by buildings, there is nothing you can do. Avoid growing crops bearing fruit or pods, and try vegetables which produce leaves and roots, and those which mature very quickly. If the shade is produced by trees and shrubs, these can be removed or thinned to admit more light.

Shelter

Windy sites may cause physical damage and will put the plants under stress while they are establishing. It can also prevent insects from flying, resulting in little or no pollination, which is essential to crops such as runner and broad beans.

What can I do if my garden is very windy?
You can erect or plant some form of windbreak, which reduces or filters the wind.

The idea is to try to reduce the speed of the wind, rather than stop it entirely. A solid windbreak, such as a wall, causes a deflection of the airstream and creates an area of low pressure on the leeward side of the windbreak. The result is severe turbulence, which can cause more damage than the original wind.

Solid wall or fence

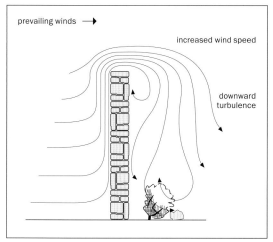

prevailing winds →

increased wind speed

downward turbulence

A wind-filtering hedge

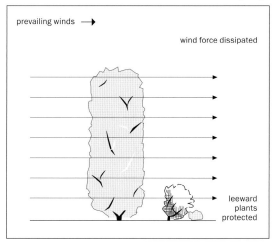

prevailing winds →

wind force dissipated

leeward plants protected

The way to overcome this is to use a semi-permeable barrier, such as a hedge or screen. A windbreak with 50 per cent permeability gives reasonable protection for a distance of up to ten times its height, and this corresponds to the distance over which the crop yield is affected.

My present vegetable plot is surrounded by a larch lap fence, which allows some wind to pass through it. Any living or non-living material can be used to make a windbreak providing it reduces the wind speed and does not cause turbulence.

The advantages of a windbreak in the vegetable garden are:

~ It reduces the likelihood of soil drying out. A moist soil is especially important when seeds are germinating.

~ It helps maintain a higher temperature around the plants. In a sheltered area, temperatures can be raised by 0.5°C (1°F).

~ It prevents physical damage to crops that are sensitive to wind, such as runner beans.

~ It reduces the amount of water loss due to transpiration. Water is drawn out of plants by high winds. Plants with water stress have reduced growth and do not produce large numbers of flowers (and without flowers there is nothing for the bees to pollinate and fertilise, and so no vegetables).

~ It increases the number of pollinating insects. Insects find it difficult to fly if the site is windy and are more likely to come to a sheltered spot.

For all these reasons, a sheltered site should lead to higher yields.

What can I do if my plot is prone to frost?
Tender crops such as runner beans and tomatoes are easily damaged by frost, so choose a sheltered spot and avoid frost pockets if possible.

You can identify a frost pocket by going out into the garden following a frost. Sometimes you will notice that frost remains on parts of the plot long after it has lifted everywhere else. These areas are known as frost pockets and will be colder in the spring than areas where the frost lifts first.

If your plot is prone to frost, wait until the last frost has passed before sowing outdoors, or sow under the protection of a cloche or in a greenhouse (see page 55). Keep an eye on your weather conditions by looking at the BBC website or listening to local radio, or take advice from fellow gardeners.

Accessibility
When planning your vegetable garden, remember that you will need room to manoeuvre a wheelbarrow around your plot, or perhaps take delivery of a large load of manure. Think about how you will do this, and allow space for such deliveries.

Availability of water
Water is essential for growing any crop, so install plenty of water butts at various locations around the site, or get a long hose, attached to the mains supply from your house.

A neat and tidy plot helps to reduce problems with the build-up of pests and diseases and also reduces the number of overwintering sites for them.

Firm pathways give good accessibility for wheelbarrows and allow the maximum use of land.

Christine's tips

SOIL TYPE

Soils vary according to the nature of the rocks from which they are formed, so different parts of the country tend to have different types of soil, and these have various advantages and disadvantages.

Vegetables will grow satisfactorily on nearly all soil provided it is properly managed. The ideal soil has a medium to heavy texture and is well drained (see page 18), but holds enough plant food for satisfactory growth, and enough lime to maintain a suitable pH (see page 17). It should be moist but not wet. This soil is rare.

Whatever your soil type, make use of its advantages and improve it as necessary. I have a light sandy loam which means that it does not hold water at all, so I add a large amount of organic matter every winter in an attempt to improve its moisture-retentive ability. This also adds a small amount of plant nutrients. Once the crops are harvested I sow a green manure (see page 36) and turn this in when I do my digging.

How do I find out what type of soil I have?

The easiest way to find out more about your soil is to look at it and feel it. Examine the top 8–10cm (3–4in) and work through the following questions:

1. Is the soil very stony?
If there are more than 20 stones on the surface per square metre (square yard), you have stony soil.

2. What colour is the soil?
If it is black or dark brown in colour and feels spongy, it is peaty soil; if not, go to the next question.

Different types of soil

Stony soils are usually free draining and easy to work in the spring. However, they dry out very quickly, nutrients are easily washed out and they can be difficult to cultivate. Root crops may develop 'fangs'. It is a waste of time to remove any but the largest stones from the surface.

Peaty soils are easy to work but you will need to check the pH every year (see page 17) to ensure good nutrient availability. They may be too acid for some crops, and may be poorly drained in winter.

The light soils (sands and loamy sands) have an open texture, making them easy to work and free draining. Because they do not retain a lot of water, they warm up sooner than the heavy soils in spring, but they cool down rapidly at night. They are hungry soils, requiring regular feeding, and they also need regular watering in the summer if they dry out due to lack of rain. In a drought situation shallow-rooted plants may die.

The medium soils (medium loam) generally have a good crumb structure with good water- and food-holding properties. However, they may cap (see page 50) under very wet conditions.

The heavy soils (heavy loam and clay soils) are usually well supplied with plant foods which do not wash away easily. However, they can be cold soils in the spring because of the amount of water they hold, making them unsuitable for early crops. They can be very heavy to work when wet and tend to become waterlogged in winter but may cake hard and crack in dry conditions.

3. Take a small amount of damp soil (about an eggcup-full) and knead it with your fingers.

a) *Does it feel gritty?* Grit is angular and sharp, and it 'jumps' as you roll it in your fingers. *Does it feel sandy?* Sandy soil feels like pieces of granulated sugar being rolled through your fingers. In either case, if the answer is yes, you have a light soil; if the answer is no, move on to the next question.

b) *Does it feel sticky?* If it doesn't feel sticky, the soil is a medium loam; if it feels sticky, move on to the next question.

c) *Does it look shiny when you make it into a ball and drag your thumb over the surface?* If the answer is yes, you have a clay or clay loam soil; if the answer is no, you have a heavy loam.

SOIL pH

Soil pH is the degree of acidity or alkalinity of a soil. It is measured on a scale of 0 to 14. A pH of 7 is neutral; below 7 is acid and above 7 is alkaline.

As the pH varies, the availability of plant nutrients increases or decreases (see diagram). Most plants can be grown in a soil with a pH in the range 6–7, but the wider the band in the chart, the more available the nutrients. At a pH of 6.5 all of the nutrients the plant needs are available for it to use.

If the soil pH is on the side of acid at 5, nitrogen, phosphorus, potassium, calcium and magnesium will be present in small amounts, which can result in plant deficiency symptoms (see page 40). In this same soil, iron, manganese, boron, copper and zinc become so readily available that there may be a toxicity problem.

Most vegetables grow well at a pH of 6.5. Members of the brassica family, such as broccoli, Brussels sprouts, cabbage and cauliflower, prefer a more alkaline soil with a pH of 7–7.5. This lessens the chance of clubroot attacking the plants (see page 99).

Availability of nutrients at different pH values

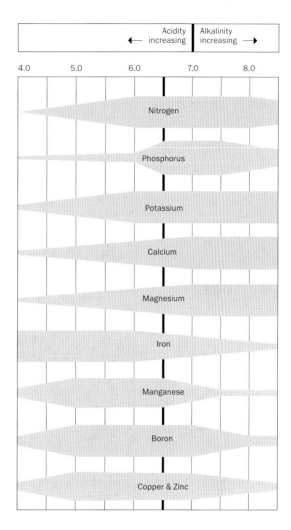

How can I test for pH?

Obtain a simple kit from a garden centre or from your horticultural or allotment society, and follow the instructions. Ideally you should do this every year.

It is important to collect a representative sample of soil when you test the pH level because several factors can have an effect on the reading. For example, taking soil from the site of a bonfire will not be representative of the soil surrounding the fire. And soil which contains fertiliser residues will give a lower pH reading than soil which does not, especially if the fertiliser contained sulphates.

The best way to collect soil for testing is to walk over your site in a W-shaped pattern and dig samples at roughly evenly spaced points (see below), placing the samples in a plastic bag. Remove any worms, twigs or stones and mix the samples together thoroughly.

Keep the containers in which you test the soil clean or errors can occur, and remember the indicator dye or powder used in soil test kits can deteriorate with storage. When you test your sample you will end up with a coloured solution which you place against a coloured chart. This tells you the pH level of your soil and whether you need to correct it or not.

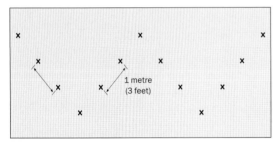

Technique for collecting soil samples for pH testing

How to correct soil acidity

Most soils in Britain tend to become acid due to rainwater continually passing through the soil and washing the lime out. Excessive soil acidity may be corrected by the application of lime (which is a form of calcium, and alkaline), but this should be done only when really necessary. In the past, gardeners tended to apply lime when it was not needed, resulting in over-liming, which makes certain nutrients unavailable to the plant. I test my soil with a pH kit every year and only apply lime if I need to.

The amount of lime to use will be influenced by the crops which you wish to grow, the soil type and the present pH. I suggest you follow the recommendations given on the pH test kit and the packet of lime.

How do I apply lime? Apply the lime with a spade from either a bucket or a wheelbarrow, scattering it evenly over the surface of the soil. Never handle the lime with your bare hands as it can burn. If any lime gets in your eyes seek medical attention immediately and make sure that you wash your hands and face after application.

When do I apply lime? Apply lime in the autumn or immediately after winter digging, so that the rain slowly dissolves it into the soil. Never apply it at the same time as you add manure or fertiliser, because the two can react and lose their effectiveness or give off ammonia, which can damage plants. It can take up to six months for lime to rectify acidity.

How to correct soil alkalinity

Few vegetables will grow in an over-alkaline soil with a pH above 8. This pH level is not common in the British Isles, but it can be difficult to correct.

One way to reduce alkalinity is to apply powdered sulphur at a rate of 130g per sq m (4½ oz per sq yd) in the autumn, forking it into the soil or sprinkling it on top. Be careful not to overdo the application of sulphur as you may cause damage to the micro-organisms in the soil.

Acidifying fertilisers, such as ammonium sulphate, will also help. Avoid using fertilisers which contain calcium, such as Nitrochalk, as these will make the soil more alkaline.

DRAINAGE

Why is drainage important?

Plants need water for growth and development and to enable plant nutrients to be taken into the plant, but too much water is not good for them.

When soil is poorly drained, excess water stays in the soil and becomes stagnant, instead of draining away into the subsoil. Stagnant water lacks the oxygen essential for plants to grow and also allows the build-up of harmful bacteria and other toxic materials, so poor drainage often results in less than satisfactory growth, and may even lead to death of plants.

The major advantages of good drainage:

~ The soil tends to warm up faster in the spring and so earlier sowings can be made.

~ Good drainage improves soil aeration, allowing the exchange of oxygen which is essential for good plant growth, and the dissipation of toxic gases from the soil.

~ When excess soil moisture is removed there is a greater depth of soil suitable for root penetration and growth.

~ Deeper rooting enables plants to 'search' and obtain more water in summer. This reduces the need for watering during drought periods.

~ There is a better distribution of plant nutrients throughout the soil.

How well drained is your soil?

It is important to know what the drainage in your soil is like. You can find this out simply by digging a hole. Use a spade to dig a hole about 1 x 1m (3 x 3ft) square and 1m (3ft) deep, at the lowest part of your plot. (I know it's difficult, but doing this will save you problems in the long term.) The hole will provide you with a vertical face or profile of the soil and will give you some indication of what the soil is like at a depth of 1m (3ft). The layer of soil at this depth is called subsoil.

It is possible to get a good idea of how well the soil is drained from certain signs in the soil profile. The colour of the various layers of soil (or horizons) shows whether the soil is drained sufficiently. If each horizon is brightly coloured without any mottling, then the soil is well drained. Dull colours and mottling show inadequate drainage.

The presence of grey colours, known as gleying, also indicates poor drainage. The relative proportions of the grey to rust colours show how bad the drainage is, and the depth and intensity of the gleying will show which horizon is impermeable to water. If the soil has a compacted layer but is slowly permeable to water, then the gleying usually occurs within it and above it.

Look at the hole to see if you can recognise any problems. If nothing jumps out at you then you're in luck and you will be able to grow your vegetables without having to consider improving the drainage.

After about a week or so of heavy rain, go and have a look at the hole and see how much water is present, if any. If the soil is well drained all the water will have drained away.

Improving the drainage

If your plot is not well drained, the best option is to make a tile drain system. Channels are dug in the plot and a herringbone pattern of plastic pipes is laid in them, which drain to a discharge point. Rubble is placed on top of the pipes before the topsoil is replaced. However, being realistic, very few of us can afford to do this or have the necessary knowledge to install such a system ourselves.

In practice, we are more likely to dig a soakaway system at the lowest part of the garden to collect surplus water. Dig a hole as deep and as large as you can and fill this with coarse rubble. The water will collect at this point.

Raising the level of the soil by as little as 30cm (12in) can have a marked beneficial effect on an area that is wet, so creating raised beds is another option (see page 29). Alternatively, consider growing your crops in pots or containers (see page 32). Simplest of all, dig in regular applications of organic matter as this will slowly improve the soil's drainage over time.

DIGGING

Why do I need to dig?

Although digging is often considered to be one of the hardest jobs in the garden, I do not think it such. I enjoy the rhythm of digging and the satisfaction of ensuring that the plants will have the best start next season. I like getting warm on a chilly day and seeing the results of my turning the soil over and burying any material that I wish to.

Digging is used to incorporate manure or other organic matter, and to control weeds. It also relieves compaction and exposes a greater surface area to frost and weathering, which helps produce a good tilth (see page 49).

Can I do something else instead? When growing vegetables in raised beds (see page 29) you can follow the no-digging method and apply a layer of well-rotted compost or other organic matter to the surface each year. The insects and worms then incorporate this into the soil over a period of time. Seeds are sown into this well-rotted layer.

However, in my experience this method is not suitable in the normal plot, where digging is essential if you are growing vegetables. Without it, weeds build up and compaction can make it difficult to produce a suitable tilth in the spring when seed sowing.

How can I make digging easier?

Make life easier for yourself by remembering the following tips:

~ Get yourself a spade which is not too heavy and feels well balanced. Ladies' spades are smaller than a standard digging spade and you may find one of these easier to handle.

~ If your soil is very stony, heavy or sticky, even when it is fairly dry, use a fork instead of a spade. You will find it much easier.

~ Use the full depth of the spade's blade (called a spit). Push it in vertically, lever the spade backwards to get the soil on the blade, and then lift it and turn the soil right over into the trench in front of you.

~ Don't take great wedges of soil at a time but instead take thin slices.

~ Work in strips, taking out a trench and then turning the soil from the trench you are working on into the one in front.

~ Don't overdo it. I find it is better to work slowly but steadily and allow your muscles to get used to the work. Don't attempt too much at once. If you have a large plot of land, divide it up into sections.

~ The best time to dig a heavy soil is in the autumn, when it can be left to weather: the rain, frosts and freezing and thawing action will help to break down the soil. Do not dig if the soil is wet or sticky, to avoid causing compaction.

~ Dig light soils in the late winter and early spring, so they do not settle too much and become compacted before you attempt to prepare the ground in the spring.

Always add as much organic matter to your soil as possible. This will help to maintain its structure and productivity.

Christine's tip

Single digging

(also known as ordinary digging)

Like most vegetable gardeners, I single dig my own vegetable garden each year, incorporating substantial amounts of compost and manure when I can get it. I do this in January or February as I am on a light soil.

Simply turning the soil over is not digging and does not have the benefits of digging. The advantages of proper single and double digging are exactly the same as you would achieve by ploughing the plot.

~ Dig out the first trench, to the depth of the spade blade and about 30cm (12in) wide, and carry the soil to the back of the plot.

~ Spread as much manure or compost as possible along the trench, adding at least a builder's bucketful per metre (yard) run of trench, and turn the next strip of soil into the trench in front of you, on top of the manure or compost.

~ Carry on until you come to the end of the plot, then use the soil from the first trench to fill in the last trench.

Single digging

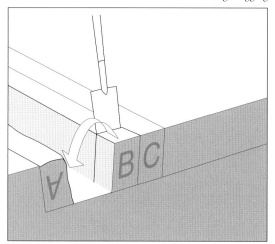

Double digging

When double digging, the ground is cultivated to a depth of two spade blades (or spits), though a fork is used on the lower layer. Because double digging breaks up the soil to a far greater depth than any other form of digging or rotavating, this method is used on land that has not been cultivated before. It is repeated every four or five years, to remove any compaction that may have developed.

~ Dig out a trench as above but make the trench wider, about 45cm (18in). Take the soil to the other end of the plot.

~ Take a fork and turn over the bottom of the trench, using the full length of the fork's prongs.

~ Spread manure or compost at the bottom of the trench, and then turn over the next strip into the trench in front of you, on top of the manure or compost.

~ Fork over the trench bottom left by removing soil from the second trench and add manure or compost.

~ Continue along the plot until you reach the last trench, then put the soil from the first trench into the last trench.

Double digging

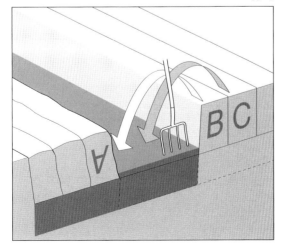

Incorporating grass and annual weeds

Double digging can also be used to clear a plot of weeds. You can bury the annual weeds, but should remove all perennial weeds as you work forward.

~ Skim off the surface grass and weeds and put these into a wheelbarrow.

~ Dig out the first trench, as for single digging, and carry the soil to the back of the plot.

~ Fork over the soil at the bottom of the trench, as described above.

~ Place the weeds and grass on top of the forked-over trench.

~ With a spade, turn over the next trench, on top of the weeds, and continue as described above.

Rotary cultivators

A rotary cultivator (or rotavator) is not a reliable substitute for digging, so do not be tempted to use one instead of digging every year. The machine may smash the soil particles into small fragments and these tend to settle out into individual components when they are wet, causing panning (a pan is a layer of soil that is very compacted).

A rotavator can also cause something known as a rotavator pan. This is a layer of smeared soil (see page 172) at the level where the blades cut through the soil at the lowest point.

However, a rotavator can be used for the incorporation of surface rubbish and weeds, and there are different blade types available for different jobs. For example, a ridging body can be used for earthing up vegetables such as celery, leeks and potatoes.

Before using a rotavator with any of its blades, check soil conditions are correct, otherwise you will do more harm than good. This is especially true of the L-shaped blade.

chapter 2

USING THE SITE

DOs AND DON'Ts

Small gardens (less than 5sq m/6sq yd) or no garden at all

If you have no garden at all, sow a few seeds in a plant pot, container, window box or grow bag. It is so easy that it is a pity not to gain all the benefits of growing just a few crops even if you only have limited room. In a small garden:

Do

~ Grow quick-maturing crops such as salad vegetables to get the most out of your plot.

~ Grow compact cultivars that need less space:

Beetroot 'Pablo' F1 hybrid
Broad bean 'The Sutton'
Cabbage 'Minicole', 'Redcap' F1 hybrid
Carrot 'Atlas'
Courgette 'Midnight' F1 hybrid, 'Tuscany'
Lettuce 'Mini Green Improved'
Potato 'Lady Christl', 'Juliette'
Salad leaves 'Baby Leaf Salad Mix', 'Spicy Green Mix'
Spinach 'Florana' F1 hybrid
Spring onion 'White Lisbon'
Tomato 'Tumbling Tom Red', 'Totem' F1 hybrid

~ Buy only a few plants from a garden centre or sow only a few seeds from the packet at any one time.

~ Carry out catch cropping and successional sowing (see page 30).

~ Pay particular attention to manual control of weeds as using chemicals on a very small scale is impractical and expensive.

Don't

~ Grow long-maturing crops such as Brussels sprouts or purple or white cultivars of broccoli.

~ Plant the area with large plants, as there will be room for so few of them and nothing else.

~ Sow all your seeds at once. If you do, you will have nowhere to plant the seedlings and you will have to give some of them away or throw them on the compost heap. Divide the packet up and save some of the seeds for next year (see page 46).

~ Sow seeds or try to grow plants in containers that are too shallow. These will dry out very quickly and will need almost continuous feeding and watering. For salad crops a very minimum of 6–10cm (2½–4in) is required and for other vegetables a minimum of 30cm (12in) will make your life and looking after the crop much easier. Greater depth is beneficial in lots of ways.

~ Buy large quantities of fertiliser or other chemicals unless you have room to store them properly, as they may go hard once opened, or break down and become inactive.

~ Have excessively wide paths, as this reduces your cropping area.

DOs AND DON'Ts

Medium gardens (5–10sq m/6–12sq yd)

In a medium-sized garden you can do all the things suggested for small gardens, as well as following the recommendations here. More space allows you to cultivate a greater range of crops.

Do

~ Consider planting or erecting some form of shelter if your garden is exposed (see page 12).

~ Set up a compost bin or heap and compost as much as possible, including all your kitchen peelings as well as garden waste (see page 38).

~ Carry out crop rotation (see page 28).

~ Use mulches wherever possible, to reduce the need to water in dry weather (see page 67). This will also help control weeds.

~ Raise your own plants. It's great fun and money-saving too!

~ Buy larger quantities of fertilisers and other chemicals, or find out if the horticultural or allotment society you have joined sells garden chemicals and equipment, as they are often cheaper than shop-bought products.

~ Remember to do some stretching exercises before carrying out any digging or heavy work as a warm-up to prevent pulled muscles.

~ Join a horticultural or allotment society. They are a great place to learn from others, gain knowledge and share a sense of camaraderie, as well as swop plants.

Don't

~ Cultivate the soil when it's too wet. If it sticks to your boots, it's too wet.

~ Leave piles of rubbish and weeds lying around over winter, as they can provide an overwintering site for pests and diseases.

~ Try to clear and cultivate your plot in one go (which can be daunting, as well as being far too tiring). Concentrate on preparing and planting a small section to begin with. Seeing your success in the early stages will spur you on.

Don't worry if you don't have room for a greenhouse – I sow all my half-hardy seeds in pots on my dining-room table

CROP ROTATION

Crop rotation is a system of varying the crops that are grown on a piece of land each year. The plot is subdivided into sections and a different crop is grown in each section, with no member of a vegetable family being grown in the same section more than once every three years.

This is primarily a method of controlling pests and diseases. Different diseases tend to affect different plant families. For example, clubroot can occur in brassicas but not in potatoes, and scab disease of potatoes affects potatoes but not broad beans. Moving the crops each year helps prevent a build-up of any problems. Crop rotation also ensures the correct fertilisers and manure are used and regular liming takes place, if needed.

A three-year rotation

Divide the plot into three sections and divide the vegetables you want to grow into three groups:

Legumes: beans and peas; and miscellaneous crops: aubergine, celery, cucumber, leek, lettuce, marrow, onion and tomato

Root crops: beetroot, carrot, parsnip, potato, swede and turnip

Leaf crops: brassicas, such as Brussels sprouts, cabbage, cauliflower and kale; and salad crops

Each group of vegetables will be growing in one of the three different sections of the plot, and they are grown in a different place each year, returning to their first growing place at the end of the third year, when the three-year cycle recommences (see below). Do not plant vegetables from different groups in the same part of the plot.

Before sowing or planting, prepare the different sections of the plot for the group that is going to be growing there. For the legumes and miscellaneous crops, supply well-rotted manure or garden compost; for the root crops, apply fertiliser; and for the brassicas and salad crops, dig in fertiliser and lime (add lime in the autumn and fertiliser in the spring).

Are there any exceptions to rotation? It is impractical to rotate the crops on small plots such as mine. All I have done for the last forty years is to move the vegetables around, so that I never grow the same crop in the same place two years running.

Sometimes I do not have enough room for everything, so I also use containers. Growing different crops in the containers every year has the same effect as rotating crops in the ground.

The other exception is perennial crops, such as asparagus, globe artichoke and herbs, which are best grown in their own beds. If your garden is big enough, grow them in an area which will not upset or interfere with your rotation plan.

Crop plan for year one

Grow root crops here

Grow leaf crops here

Grow legumes and miscellaneous crops here

Crop plan for year two

Grow legumes and miscellaneous crops here

Grow root crops here

Grow leaf crops here

Crop plan for year three

Grow leaf crops here

Grow legumes and miscellaneous crops here

Grow root crops here

THE BED SYSTEM

In a bed system, the soil is placed into raised beds which sit above the ground and are separated by permanent paths. Ideally, make your beds 1–1.2m (3–4ft) wide, with a minimum depth of 20cm (8in).

Dig the beds thoroughly when you first make them, to break up any compaction. After that you add organic matter each year but there is no need to dig it in. You can rotate the crops in different beds.

The advantages of the bed system are:

~ All work is carried out from the path, thus preventing the damage to the soil structure that is caused by walking on it, and reducing compaction.

~ The roots of all crops can penetrate deeper than normal, due to the lack of compaction, which gives a higher yield per unit.

~ Drainage is improved because of the lack of compaction.

~ You cultivate, fertilise and manure only the beds, not the paths, saving time and money.

~ Spacing in a raised bed is generally closer than in the ground, so most of the crops grow to form a canopy over the soil, thus smothering weed growth.

~ Weed growth on the paths can be easily controlled with weedkillers or mulches (see page 164).

TECHNIQUES IDEAL FOR SMALL GARDENS

Catch cropping

With this technique, you grow quick-maturing vegetables such as endive, lettuce, radishes and spring onions in the gaps which remain after you have removed a slower-growing vegetable and before you plant another. For example, if you remove peas you can sow radishes in the same space before you plant the area with cabbages. Likewise, once the first crops from a spring sowing have been harvested, sow or plant corn salad, winter radishes or endive in that vacant land before planting a slower-growing crop. Here are a few examples:

~ Carrots, followed by spring onions or leeks
~ Garlic overwintered, followed by French beans
~ Beetroot, followed by lettuce and endive
~ Peas, followed by beetroot
~ First potatoes, followed by calabrese
~ Broad beans sown from mid- to late autumn, followed by leeks
~ Spring cabbage, followed by potatoes or leeks
~ Lettuce sown in mid-spring, followed by swedes or French beans

~ Onions planted in mid-spring, followed by winter radishes, lettuce or kale
~ Cabbage overwintered, followed by potatoes, leeks or any of the salad vegetables
~ Spinach sown in mid-spring, followed by celeriac
~ Carrots, followed by beetroot and endive
~ First early potatoes, followed by leeks

Combined cropping

Here two crops are grown together in the same row: for example, onions between carrots. The idea is that the onions will be given more space to grow and mature as the carrots are pulled. For the same reason, lettuce and other salads may be grown with a brassica such as Brussels sprouts, and radishes and parsnips may be sown at the same time as each other.

Successional sowing

This type of cropping relies on frequent sowings taking place so that you get a steady supply of vegetables over a long period of time. Radishes sown every 7–10 days will give you a long period of supply, as will lettuce sown every 10 days.

Combined cropping

Successional sowing

Intercropping

Intercropping is very similar to combined cropping except that you grow a quick-maturing crop in the gaps between rows of wider-spaced and generally slower-growing crops. For example, lettuce can be grown between rows of peas, or radishes between rows of potatoes.

Continuity of varieties

During the growing season you will find that there are periods when you have too many vegetables and others when you only have a few. Gluts can be avoided by successive sowing as described above, and by sowing little and often. There tends to be a gap in the supply of vegetables from late winter through to about late spring, but if you plant and choose your varieties carefully and plant at the right time, certain crops such as Brussels sprouts, kale, leeks, spinach, spring cabbage, sprouting broccoli, turnips and winter cauliflowers will mature during this time.

Intercropping

Planning your crops

People often ask me how I get my vegetables to be ready for when I am at home, as I travel a lot and am not home at all some weeks. This is down to timing.

Below is a list of the approximate number of weeks it will take for crops to mature, from seed sowing to harvest. (This will vary depending on where you live in Britain, your soil type and how you grow your crops.) For a crop in, say, early autumn, I count backwards the number of weeks the crop will need, and sow as close to this date as possible.

Aubergines	20–22 weeks
Beetroot	12–16 weeks
Broad beans	14–28 weeks
Broccoli	12–16 weeks
Brussels sprouts	28–35 weeks
Cabbage	10–26 weeks
Capsicums (peppers)	18–20 weeks
Carrots	12–20 weeks
Cauliflower	20–46 weeks
Celery	18–30 weeks
Corn salad	16 weeks
Courgettes and marrows	10–14 weeks
Cucumbers	14–18 weeks
Early potatoes	13–16 weeks
French beans	8–12 weeks
Leeks	30–45 weeks
Lettuce	4–14 weeks
Parsnips	34 weeks
Peas	14–32 weeks
Pumpkins and squash	14–20 weeks
Radishes	3–12 weeks
Runner beans	12–14 weeks
Shallots	18–28 weeks
Spinach	8–14 weeks
Spring onions	10 weeks
Sprouting broccoli	35–40 weeks
Tomatoes	15–17 weeks

GROWING IN CONTAINERS

Practically any container of any shape may be used to grow vegetables. I have seen old fish boxes, guttering, half barrels, old sinks, washing-up bowls, strawberry pots, grow bags, tyres, Cretan jars, potato barrels, hanging baskets, window boxes, wheelbarrows and buckets, to name a few, supporting healthy crops.

However, very shallow containers will restrict what you can grow: the soil dries out very quickly and there is little room for root growth. A seedtray with about 6cm (2½in) depth of soil may be used for growing salad leaves, but will not support the long-term growth of, say, leeks or carrots. A window box should be at least 15cm (6in) deep and wide to prevent rapid drying out on a daily basis in hot, sunny weather.

Compost or soil

It is false economy to use an inferior soil or compost to fill a container. I would recommend a high-quality multi-purpose compost or a John Innes No.2 for vegetable growing.

I am often asked if it's OK to just replace half of the soil with new compost each spring. In my opinion, the answer is no. In large containers I replace the soil completely every three years and in smaller pots, troughs and window boxes I change the soil every year. Replace the whole lot if you can, and most certainly if you have had any pest or disease on your crops.

Watering

The aim should be to water the entire content of the container each time you do so. To achieve this, you may have to water the container, let it drain, water it again, let it drain and water it again.

Remember that once plants are growing in the container their leaves will shed most of the rain water, resulting in very little actually getting to the soil, let alone any deeper, even in heavy rain.

Hanging baskets make great containers for growing vegetables, especially salad crops, but the basket will need attending to every day to ensure that it does not dry out. Daily watering may be needed during the summer. This is easier if you use a spring-loaded pulley mechanism which allows the basket to be lowered and raised, or use a hand lance fitted to the end of a hosepipe.

Every container should be:

Clean Old soil on the container's sides may carry soil-borne diseases which can infect new soil and crops.

Stable Tall, thin containers may be blown over: a wide base gives greater stability.

Reasonably deep The shallower the container, the quicker it will dry out in the summer. The minimum depth for each crop has been given in the relevant chapter.

Frost proof This is essential if the container will be outside all winter. When growing long-term crops like Brussels sprouts or leeks, you do not want frost to split the container open.

Adequately drained The container may become waterlogged if it does not have drainage holes. If you have to make them, they should be at least 1cm (½in) in diameter and 15cm (6in) apart. To prevent compost falling through the holes, put a layer of fine netting over them. I find old net curtains great for this job. Standing the container on feet will prevent drainage holes being sealed while on the ground.

Not too full Allow a gap of at least 4cm (1½in) between the top of the soil or compost and the top of the container, so that you can apply enough water to wet its volume without most of it running off the surface.

Many seed companies offer patio, mini or container vegetables which are suitable for small plots or if you live on your own. If the only place you want to grow vegetables is in a container, just refer to that section in the seed catalogues.

A simple test to find out the dampness of the soil is to push your index finger into the middle of the container and feel how wet or dry it is.

Christine's tips

chapter 3

FEEDING

Manures, composts and fertilisers

MANURE AND OTHER ORGANIC MATTER

What is manure and organic matter?

Organic matter is anything which is derived from an animal or vegetable, while manure is generally a bulky material derived from animals.

As organic matter breaks down it becomes humus, which is vital because it contains and maintains living organisms such as bacteria in the soil. Bacteria break down the complex chemicals in organic matter into simple plant food which plants can absorb.

Sources of bulky organic matter include farmyard manure, horse manure, compost, leaf mould, mushroom compost, poultry manure, sawdust, seaweed, spent hops, straw, the contents of old grow bags and spent potting compost.

Animal manures, for example cow or horse manure, should always be stacked for 6–12 months, allowing time for the material to break down before being dug into the soil. Fresh manure can release strong ammonia and other chemicals that can cause damage to the roots of plants.

How can organic matter improve my soil?

Manure, compost and other organic matter are very bulky, and their main use is to improve the structure of the soil. They will also improve the soil's fertility and supply nutrients. Improving the soil structure by regular applications of organic matter has the following effects:

Better water-holding capacity This is particularly important on a light, sandy soil, which tends to be well drained, but is helpful on any soil, particularly in times of drought.

Easier root penetration Most root vegetables, such as parsnips and carrots, can grow longer more easily.

Better drainage On clay soils, organic matter helps to bind soil particles together, causing them to make larger granules which allows easier drainage.

Garden compost

Mushroom compost

Farmyard manure

Leaf mould

The overall effect is that nutrients are held by organic matter and thus leaching (washing away) is avoided. In addition, soils which contain a high percentage of organic matter are darker, absorb more of the sun's radiant heat, and are therefore warmer in the spring, enabling you to start seed sowing and planting earlier.

Green manure

If you do not have access to the traditional sources of manure listed above, consider supplying some organic matter to your garden in the form of a green manure. This can be produced by sowing the seeds of a suitable plant into vacant soil and then digging the plant into the soil once it has grown.

Suitable plants include buckwheat, red and white clover, fenugreek, lupins, mustard and *Phacelia tanacetifolia*, plus many others, and seed is sold in garden centres and seed catalogues.

Types of green manure

Alfalfa Does not do well on an acid soil but prefers an alkaline one, and it will not tolerate wet soils. If put down as a long-term manure, for say a year or more, you can remove the top growth and put this on the compost heap, leaving about 8cm (3in) of growth on the plant to regrow.

Bitter blue lupins A deep-rooted leguminous plant that thrives on acid soils. Not dense growth so keep weed free.

Buckwheat Grows rapidly on poor soils and may be used as a short-term manure. Sow only when the soil has warmed up. Attractive to beneficial insects.

Crimson clover Prefers a light soil but I have seen it growing well on heavy ones. Sow in mid-summer to allow it to establish before the winter. If sown late in cold regions it does not grow very well.

Essex red clover Prefers a fertile soil and will not be successful on acid soils. Dig in during the spring. This crop may be left in situ for up to a year before being dug in.

White clover Best used as a long-term manure where it can be sown as a living mulch, sown between rows of other long-term crops. Sometimes mixed with perennial ryegrass.

Fenugreek Does well on well-drained soils and is reasonably drought tolerant once established. The young leaves may be eaten. It is fast growing. Do not sow before the ground has warmed up.

Fodder radish Grows well on all soil types. Frost causes the plans to rot off which makes it a good crop

Buckwheat   *Phacelia tanacetifolia*

for the winter. A useful alternative to mustard when clubroot may be a problem.

Grazing rye One of the best overwintering green manures. Often mixed with vetches. Reports state that it may suppress wireworms. Suitable for most soils.

Mustard Do not grow on land infected with clubroot. Grows well on most fertile soils. Very fast growing. Cut down after flowering for maximum bulk. May be turned in after three weeks if necessary.

Phacelia tanacetifolia Will grow on all soil types. A leafy quick-growing crop. Will tolerate a light frost. It is very attractive to bees. Do not sow any later than August.

Trefoil Does not grow well on acid soils, but is useful in dappled shade and will also grow on light dry soils. This is a biennial crop that may be left for a whole season if required.

Winter tares Best sown on heavy soils and not very tolerant of drought. Sow in September. I often cut this down in the spring and put the top growth on my compost heap and let it regrow before turning it in. The plant is attractive to bees.

Green manures are not a substitute for bulky organic matter, but are very useful to fill an empty space, particularly in winter. Depending on the plant used, the benefits of a green manure are that it:

~ protects the soil surface from heavy rain
~ suppresses weed growth
~ adds organic matter to the soil
~ releases nutrients for the next crop, once dug in
~ improves soil structure (though not all do this)
~ helps the soil retain moisture
~ attracts beneficial insects, if it is a flowering crop
~ increases the available nitrogen in the soil

It is important to ensure that you select the correct green manure for your own soil and conditions. It is worth sowing a small amount of many different types at first, to see which does the best. Once you have established this then stick with that plant.

I have a light soil and use mustard and *Phacelia* a lot. My experience with the clovers is that they can be a nuisance if not dug in properly. They should be fully buried otherwise they stay on the surface, flower, produce seed and then seed themselves around, becoming difficult to control.

Making your own compost

I am a great believer in feeding the soil not the plant, which means I use a lot of organic matter. Since organic matter is so good for your garden, try to obtain as much of it as you can. One very good method of doing this is by making your own compost from garden or kitchen waste, which is put on a heap or in a compost bin and left to break down.

I have several bins of different shapes and sizes and colours and I do not think the size makes a difference. What is important is that the material is mixed together and not just put in

separate layers of, say, grass clippings or annual weeds or cardboard.

What can I put in the compost bin? Materials that produce compost when broken down include soft vegetable and flower stems, leaves and soft hedge clippings. Annual weeds may be used prior to flowering and bedding plants after flowering. Grass clippings are a good source of compost but only use them if they have not been treated with weedkiller.

Household waste such as eggshells, tea leaves and vegetable peelings can be included, but never add raw or cooked food as it attracts vermin. Tear cardboard up into small pieces before mixing it in with the other material.

Don't put diseased plant material on to the compost heap, and avoid tough weeds or turnip or cabbage stalks which will take a very long time to break down. I do use twigs and prunings but always put them through a grinder first so they rot down at a similar speed to the other material in the heap.

How do I make the compost? It is very important to mix all the material together before it is put in the bin or added to the heap. I collect all my kitchen waste in a large bucket, and then once I have mowed my grass I put the peelings and the grass cuttings in a sack, mix them together and just pour it all into the bin. I repeat this until the bin is full.

Do not compact each new layer as air needs to be present to bring about the conversion to compost. The materials also need moisture, so ensure that the heap is not too dry and water if necessary. I do not turn it. I just leave it to rot down on its own.

The compost should be ready 8–12 months after the heap is made. The material at the base will be ready first and should be brown and crumbly. When emptying the bin, I take off the undecomposed stuff and put it on one side, remove the rotted compost and then just put anything that isn't ready back in the bin.

Do not put a bin in full sun as it will dry out too quickly. Also avoid dense shade, but a semi-shady spot will be fine. Put the bin on to a soil base which allows water to drain away and worms to come up into the heap from the surrounding soil.

Christine's tip

PLANT FEEDING

Plant nutrient	Needed by	Signs of deficiency	Avoiding problems	Where frequently needed
Nitrogen	Leafy crops	Small, pale green leaves, weak stems and stunted growth	Top dress in spring and summer with a nitrogen-rich fertiliser such as sulphate of ammonia	Areas of high rainfall and on well-drained, sandy soils
Phosphate	Root vegetables, young rapidly growing plants, and fruit and seed crops	Small leaves with a purplish tinge; low fruit yields, stunted roots and stems	Apply a base dressing of bonemeal in early spring or feed with superphosphate in mid-spring at the manufacturer's recommended rate	Well-drained, sandy soils
Potash	Potatoes, tomatoes and other fruiting vegetables	Poorly coloured fruit and flowers, edges of the leaves turn yellow and then brown	Apply a base dressing of sulphate of potash at the manufacturer's recommended rate in mid-spring or when symptoms appear	Well-drained, sandy soils
Calcium	All crops	Stunted growth and pale green leaves	Carry out a pH test and maintain pH at 6.5 for most crops. If the soil is above pH 6.5, apply gypsum rather than lime	Potash-rich soils and those which are acid
Magnesium	Tomatoes	Yellow or brown patches between the veins of older leaves	Apply a base dressing of fertiliser containing magnesium	Sandy, peaty and potash-rich soils

FERTILISERS

Why do I need to feed my plants?

Plants are like people. They need balanced supplies of food and water to aid their growth and development. Manures and compost feed the soil and the worms (who help break up the soil), while fertilisers feed the plant not the soil and have little effect on the worms if applied correctly. Both are essential for the successful production of healthy crops.

The major foods required by plants are nitrogen, phosphorus and potassium (usually called potash), and they are known as the major elements. They are available to plants in the form of nitrates and nitrites, phosphates and potash respectively. The next group is the intermediate elements. These are foods such as calcium and magnesium, which are needed in rather smaller amounts. The final group is the trace elements, which includes molybdenum, manganese, iron, boron, copper and sulphur. These are required in extremely small quantities.

All soils contain some mineral nutrient elements, but these are lost by various means, including bacterial activity, leaching and the removal of crops. Nutrients are replaced very slowly by nature, but as a gardener you cannot wait for this to occur so it is your job to ensure that your plants receive enough food.

How do I know if my plants need feeding?

If plants are not fed they will remain very small and stunted, and may change colour (see panel). On the other hand, if you overfeed a plant with fertiliser it will produce all leaf and no flower or fruit. The growth will become very soft and sappy, making the plant susceptible to pest and disease attack. Plants may grow tall and leggy, and will be weak and prone to being blown over. They also become sensitive to frost damage, and will not survive the winter.

Apart from looking for deficiency symptoms, one of the best ways to find out if your soil and plants need any fertilisers is to carry out a simple soil nutrient test (available from a garden centre or allotment society). This will tell you how much fertiliser, if any, to apply.

I do not use much fertiliser at all in my own garden, because I am lucky enough to have access to plenty of manure and I garden on a light soil. Instead I use green manures as soon as a crop is removed and add copious amounts of organic matter each year when I carry out my digging.

However, I do use fertilisers when I am growing in containers, which need regular feeding as the crop is growing in a restricted area and can't get its nutrients from anywhere else. I use a general liquid fertiliser for most crops but one high in potash for tomatoes.

Types of fertiliser

Compound fertilisers A compound fertiliser contains the major elements (nitrogen, phosphorus and potassium) and is balanced to provide the correct amount for the type of plant for which it is recommended. On the packet you will often see a ratio quoted, such as 6:9:7. This just means it contains 6 per cent nitrogen, 9 per cent phosphate and 7 per cent potassium. Some compounds contain the major nutrient elements in equal quantities. For example, Growmore is sold as 7:7:7.

Simple or straight fertilisers These contain just one of the major elements and are generally applied to achieve specific effects: nitrogen promotes leaf growth, phosphates root growth and potash seed, fruit and flower production. Applying sulphate of ammonia (a nitrogenous fertiliser) when growing cabbages will encourage leaf growth. Dried blood is used for green vegetables, superphosphate for root crops and sulphate of potash for legumes and tomatoes.

A few of these fertilisers contain a small amount of another element as well as the major element. Bonemeal, for example, contains 20 per cent phosphate and 4 per cent nitrogen (the figures may vary depending on source and processing method).

When should I apply fertiliser?

Fertiliser may be applied to the soil before sowing or planting, or while the plant is growing, and different gardeners use fertilisers in different ways.

To make the best use of fertiliser, remember that different crops have growing seasons of varying lengths. For quick-growing crops that have a short growing season (lettuce and radishes, for example), you need a fast-releasing fertiliser such as Growmore. Crops that grow more slowly, like Brussels sprouts, need nutrients over a longer period of time and will benefit from a slow-release fertiliser like Nitrochalk.

You can apply potash and phosphates at any time before sowing or planting, as these elements are not easily washed out of the soil. However, nitrates are soon lost from the soil by leaching. If you apply them in the autumn, they will have leached away by the time you come to sow your seeds in the spring, so the best time to apply nitrates is early spring.

What is the best way to apply fertiliser?

Fertilisers are available in many different forms, including powders, crystals, granules, liquids, tablets, sticks or small bags that can be placed in a pot or container.

Generally it is fair to say that the smaller the particle size the quicker the material will be available to the plant. All fertilisers need to be dissolved before the roots can absorb the nutrients, so liquid fertilisers work the quickest. Granules and powders are scattered on the soil and left to dissolve by the rain. It is a good idea to use gloves when applying fertiliser.

Broadcasting This method is used where large areas of ground are to be fertilised and the crop's roots are capable of absorbing the fertiliser once in the soil. To broadcast fertiliser, grab a handful and throw it evenly over the surface of the soil.

The band method Crops such as lettuce, French beans and onions which do not have an extensive root system will benefit from a band of fertiliser both below the seeds and either side of them, rather than broadcast applications. The fertiliser is placed below the seed and either side of the drill because damage can occur if you have high concentrations of nitrogen, and sometimes potash, near the seeds or young roots.

Take out a deep drill, sprinkle the fertiliser in a 5cm (2in) band at the bottom of the drill and then refill until you have the correct depth needed to sow the seed. Once sown and covered, sprinkle a band 5cm (2in) to either side of the seed row.

Base dressing Fertiliser is applied in the final stages of soil preparation, before sowing or planting. The application rate depends on the type of fertiliser you are using. Apply it as recommended on the packet.

Top dressing Nitrates are best applied using this method, to ensure that enough nitrogen will be available throughout the life of the crop. Sprinkle powder or granular fertilisers around the base of the plant in a circle 15cm (6in) wide. Do not allow the fertiliser to touch the stem. For maximum benefit, work into a moist soil using a hoe. Alternatively, you can water the fertiliser into the soil after application.

Foliar feeding This is a very convenient way of applying fertiliser and is often used to correct a deficiency problem (see page 40). Concentrated fertiliser is diluted and applied to the leaves of the plant, giving a rapid but short-lived boost. Apply with a sprayer or a watering can with a fine rose.

Liquid feeding The fertiliser is diluted in water and applied to the soil around the base of the plant using a watering can. It is very useful as the feed is carried down to the roots, where it can be used immediately. Make sure the soil is moist before application, as the fertiliser can damage the roots in dry soil.

Are there any problems I need to know about?

Applying too much fertiliser may cause the following problems:

~ Seed may not germinate, as a high concentration of nutrients prevents the seed absorbing moisture.

~ Over-application once the plants are growing can result in too much soft sappy growth being produced at the expense of flowers and fruit.

~ High concentrations of fertiliser can burn the roots of plants and cause scorch.

~ Too much fertiliser will deter worm activity, resulting in poor soil structure.

Always carry out a fertiliser test (see page 41) before making any application, to confirm it is actually needed.

Christine's tip

The following tips will help you use fertilisers correctly:

Potash

Apply potash-based fertiliser in the autumn, before digging, and use sulphate of potash rather than muriate of potash, as this will cause less damage to the roots and seedlings.

Nitrogen

When applying nitrogenous fertiliser, use only part of the amount required by the crop at seed sowing and then apply the rest as a top dressing once the plants are established.

Do not place nitrogen in a band near the plants: it is better to spread the fertiliser between the rows so that the roots do not come into contact with high concentrations.

Watering

If rain has not fallen for three or four days after applying a granular or powdered fertiliser, rake it in and then water.

When you apply any fertiliser as a powder or granule, be careful not to allow any to fall on the leaves of the plants because if it dissolves in a small amount of water it forms a very strong solution which can damage the plant tissue. If you do get some on the plant, wash it off immediately with water.

In a drought, use a liquid fertiliser, not a granular or powder fertiliser formulation, but ensure the plants are damp at the roots before you apply it by watering them the day before.

After applying fertiliser, keep the soil moist until the seeds have germinated and come above the surface of the soil, or until the plants you have transplanted are established.

chapter 4

SOWING

Seeds, seedbed preparation and seed sowing

SEEDS

Where can I obtain good seed?

My advice is always to buy your seeds from a well-known source, whether by mail order or from a garden centre, so you know that what you are buying has the potential to grow. Seed will not germinate if it has been stored incorrectly or is too old, so check the sow-by date on the packet.

Can I collect my own seed? Collecting the seeds from your own plants is only reasonably practical for such subjects as beans, peas and sometimes onions. Good results can be obtained but there are hazards. For example, unless the seed is collected when it is fully ripe and matured the results when it is sown will be poor, and there is more chance of spreading seed-borne diseases by sowing your own seed. The seeds of F1 hybrids are not worth collecting.

It is also worth remembering that if you have limited time and attention to spend on collecting your own seed it may not be very practical or economical when you consider the price of well-graded, cleaned and (often) treated seeds from the seedsmen.

Some people like to save the seed of their show vegetables, but this is beyond the scope of this book.

How should seed be stored?

Seeds are alive and they start the process of deterioration the moment they are plucked from the plant. The way seed is stored, even when it is in unopened foil packets, will influence its ability to germinate.

Generally speaking, high temperatures and moisture cause rapid deterioration. For each 5°C (9°F) rise in temperature above 0°C (32°F), the storage life of seed is halved. And for each 1 per cent increase in seed moisture content between 5 and 14 per cent, the life of the seed is again halved. It is therefore obviously best to store seeds in a cool, dry place. The worst place to store seeds is in the kitchen or a damp garden shed.

Always store seed in an airtight, dark-coloured sandwich box with some silica gel (obtainable from chemists) added to absorb moisture, and keep it in the bottom of the fridge. Use about one teaspoon of the silica gel per 25g (1oz) of seed. In these conditions most seeds will remain viable for 3–4 years.

I have a sandwich box which I have divided into the months of the year. Once I have obtained the seed I put it into the months when it should be sown. This is a useful reminder and saves time sorting through lots of packets each time I go into the box. I put collected seed in a paper bag or envelope before adding it to the box in the fridge.

Seed also deteriorates with age, resulting in loss of viability (the period of time the seeds remain able to germinate), so it is not worth keeping seeds that have passed their sow-by date.

Do not attempt to store parsnip seed, as it deteriorates very quickly. In my experience, it is better to start with fresh parsnip seed every year.

Seed treatments Some seeds are sold coated with a special formulation of insecticides and fungicides. The dressing may be used to give a control for specific pests or diseases, or to give general protection. They are a cheap and effective method of control.

Use this type of seed in the same year as the treatment has taken place, because the treatment may affect the storage potential of that seed. Be sure to read the packet to check if the seed has been treated and always wash your hands after handling the seeds.

Testing seed for viability If you have some seed left over from last year, you can test to see if it will germinate. The best way to determine viability is to sprinkle some seeds on to damp blotting paper in a warm place. Within 2–3 weeks the seedling roots should start to grow. If none of the seeds tested produce roots it will be a waste of time sowing the rest. Most seeds will swell when placed in water, whether alive or dead, so this cannot be used as a test to see if they are alive and viable.

Aids to sowing

Seeds are usually sold in small foil packets, which can be fiddly to use, particularly if you have problems with your hands, but some seeds are also sold in forms that make them easier to handle. The number of varieties available will be more limited if you buy seed this way.

Tapes and sheets Single seeds are incorporated in tapes or sheets of tissue-like paper which dissolves when placed in soil. The sheets or tapes are put into the drill or on the soil, covered with the correct depth of soil and then watered. The seedlings do not require thinning out (see page 54) once germination and emergence have taken place because the seeds are already spaced in the tape or sheet. This is particularly useful when you want to space sow (see page 55).

Pelleted seed Individual seeds are coated with a clay-like material which disintegrates in the soil if enough moisture is present. The seeds look like tiny balls and are easy to handle. As they are sown individually, there is no need to thin them out later.

The seed should be sown at the depth stated on the packet and then kept moist until it comes through the soil. If the soil is too dry the clay-like material does not break down to allow the seed to germinate and if it is too wet the coat becomes very mushy and rotting may occur. Therefore correct moisture is extremely important.

Looking at and feeling the soil surface provides the best guide to watering pelleted seeds. As soon as the soil surface starts to dry it becomes a lighter colour than when it is wet, and it is at this stage that you should apply some more water. Repeat this until the seedlings come through the soil.

Pre-germinated or 'chitted' seed This seed has begun the process of germination and is ready for pricking out (see page 172). It is used for crops which need a lot of heat to start them off.

These seeds are available through some seed catalogues and they are sent to customers in moisture-proof packets to prevent moisture loss. You should prick them out immediately on receipt. As you are not germinating these seeds yourself, there is no need for a propagator or other special seed germination equipment.

Choosing a variety

Go to any garden centre or open a seed catalogue and you are faced with a bewildering number of varieties. If you have no idea which is best, you can follow my suggestions, or have a chat with your gardening friends or someone who belongs to the local horticultural or allotment society. They will be able to tell you which variety grows well in your area and on your soil type. Look for the following as a way of helping you choose:

AGM symbol The Royal Horticultural Society's Award of Garden Merit (AGM) indicates a variety of outstanding quality which will grow in all sorts of soil types and conditions. These plants have a strong constitution and do not require specialist care or growing conditions. One of the greatest benefits is that they are not particularly susceptible to any pests and diseases.

F1 hybrids An F1 hybrid is a plant that has been produced by cross-pollinating two parent lines which have been selected for particular characteristics for several generations. The hybrid plants produced are more vigorous than the parent plants, they tend to be more uniform in their height, colour and shape, and they often mature at the same time.

Many of these characteristics, such as improved vigour, are of particular value to the gardener, but having all the plants mature at the same time can cause problems of oversupply unless you only sow a few seeds at a time or have ample storage facilities.

Some people save the seed from F1 hybrids, only to be disappointed the following year when the plants have lost their desirable qualities. The seedsman has to breed new F₁ hybrid seed every year, which is why it costs more than ordinary varieties.

Pest and disease resistance Most seedsmen have spent a lot of time breeding resistance into newer varieties of vegetable, but many of the older ones can still come under attack. Experience in all walks of life has shown that prevention is better than cure and this theory is true for vegetable growing. It is more effective and cheaper to prevent attack than to try to cure it once it has occurred.

With the recent reduction in the number of materials permitted for the control of pests and diseases, growing the following disease-resistant varieties is an excellent way of avoiding problems:

Carrot 'Flyaway' F₁ hybrid and 'Resistafly' F₁ hybrid
~ *resistant to carrot fly*
Courgette 'Defender' F₁ hybrid
~ *resistant to cucumber mosaic virus*
Cucumber 'Brunex' and 'Cassandra'
~ *resistant to mildew*
Parsnip 'Avonresister'
~ *resistant to canker*
Potato 'Kestrel' and 'Wilja'
~ *resistant to slugs*
Swede 'Marian'
~ *highly tolerant of mildew and clubroot*

As resistant varieties are always being developed, look in your catalogues to find the latest which have been bred with these and other useful characteristics.

Treated seeds are also available (see page 46).

Carrot 'Resistafly' F₁ hybrid

Swede 'Marian'

SEEDBED PREPARATION

A seedbed is an area of land which is cultivated so that the soil particles are a suitable size for sowing seed. The size of the seedbed will be influenced by the size of the crop plants that are being grown and the number of plants you require. I grow my crops in 1m (3ft) rows, each of which usually gives enough produce for my own needs. For guidance on what you can expect from a 1m (3ft) row, see panel below.

Preparing a tilth

When the winter has passed and the soil has started to warm up it is time to get a seedbed ready for sowing. This is known as preparing a tilth. A good tilth should be fine and crumbly, with no clods of earth.

Soil types and the type of seed you will be sowing will influence the fineness of the tilth needed. Generally speaking, the finer the seed the finer the tilth should be. This ensures that the seeds are in close contact with the soil particles and are able to absorb water from the soil.

How many vegetables do I need?

To help you plan your sowing, this is what I produced from planting a 1m (3ft) long row of each crop.

Brussels sprouts	3.5kg (7½lb)
Bulb onions	3.5kg (7½lb)
Carrots	3.8kg (8¼lb)
Courgettes	4.5kg (10lb)
French beans	2kg (4½lb)
Parsnips	4.2kg (9¼lb)
Peas	2.4kg (5½lb)
Potatoes (maincrop)	5.2kg (11½lb)
Runner beans	5kg (11lb)
Spring onions	450g (1lb)
Squash	4.8kg (10½lb)
Tomatoes	4.2kg (9¼lb)

compaction.) Then re-rake the area to produce the final tilth.

To prevent the problems of capping on seedbeds, especially on silt or clay soils, prepare a coarser tilth at this final preparation stage. The crumbs will not be broken down as quickly as very small ones. Avoid over-compaction and destruction of the structure by not doing too much treading or firming. Do not walk over the soil when it is very wet or sticky.

It is important not to work the soil into a tilth if it is damp and sticky. All you do by walking on the soil while it is in this condition is to destroy its structure and cause compaction. If the soil dries in this compacted state it may become very firm and make seedling growth and development difficult.

The soil will have been broken down reasonably well by weathering during the winter, and all that should be necessary to create a tilth is to rake through the soil until a layer of crumbs forms at the surface. The largest of these should be no bigger than a pea. Work to a depth of 5–10cm (2–4in) and remove any weeds or large stones.

Applying fertiliser Next, apply a base dressing of fertiliser if it is needed (see page 41). Scatter it evenly over the surface of the seedbed and then rake it in, going no deeper than 5–10cm (2–4in). Do not apply more fertiliser than is recommended: the seeds will not germinate faster or grow better, and too much fertiliser may delay or even prevent germination.

Finishing the seedbed preparation You should now produce the final tilth as follows. First, firm the soil by treading across the seedbed in tiny steps, keeping your feet together, so that the whole seedbed is gently trodden down. (Some people suggest that you do this firming in the initial stages of seedbed preparation, before applying the fertiliser. However, I believe that doing it at this stage is adequate, and results in fewer problems with over-firming and

What is capping?

Sandy or loamy soils can be broken down easily, but silty and clay soils must be prepared more carefully, to avoid capping.

In heavy rain the very fine silt and clay particles are broken down by the power of the raindrops, causing them to settle out in different sizes and come together to form a solid mass. If this mass dries out it can form a surface cap or crust, which the young seedlings cannot force their way through. This is known as soil slumping or capping.

Capping does not prevent the germination of seeds, only their emergence. The seeds often germinate under the cap but die because they use up their food supply and strength trying to break through the very solid surface layer of soil.

Keeping the soil surface moist will reduce the mechanical strength of this layer and will enable the seeds to push their way through.

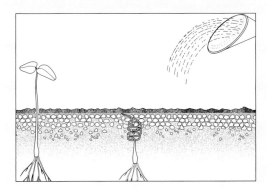

SEED SOWING

Seeds may be sown outside directly into a seedbed if they are hardy, while others which are half hardy or may be difficult to get to germinate are sown and started off under the protection of a greenhouse or on a kitchen windowsill.

I do not have a greenhouse but start most of my seeds off by sowing directly into the ground when the soil is warm enough. This is fine for the hardy ones, but not for things that require more heat to start them into growth such as runner beans. I sow these in trays on my kitchen windowsill or on my dining-room table which is pushed up against the French windows.

How can I encourage my seeds to germinate?

Here are some tips for improving the likelihood that the seeds you sow will germinate.

1. Seeds need warmth Avoid sowing seed in soil that is too cold. At temperatures of less than 5°C (41°F) the enzymes (chemical messengers) responsible for promoting the chemical changes in the seed that stimulate it to germinate do not function, and so growth does not take place.

2. Water is essential (see page 63). There needs to be enough water in the soil for the seed to absorb it. Water activates the enzymes, so without the right amount of moisture the seed just stays as it was at sowing time.

On the other hand, if the soil is too wet the seed can start to rot as it is invaded by harmful soil fungi or bacteria. In stagnant water the seed may suffocate as there will be insufficient oxygen for germination. The seed needs oxygen to enable all the chemical processes to work.

3. Soil tilth is very important (see page 49). The soil particles contain pores within which the water is held, and a fine tilth allows close contact between the seed and the soil particles. This ensures that the seed can absorb water from the soil rapidly, and growth will commence.

If the tilth is coarse and open, there will be little contact between the seed and the soil, and therefore water will not be available to the seeds for germination to take place.

4. Sowing depth is crucial (see page 52). The seed is just a food store for the young plant. It contains enough food for the seed to germinate and emerge through the soil's surface if sown at the correct depth. Once the seed reaches the light, the young plant starts to manufacture its own food by utilising sunlight in the process known as photosynthesis.

If the seed is sown too deep, the young plant will starve and wither in the soil before it reaches the surface and the light.

5. Soil-borne pests and diseases may be a problem They can prevent the seed from germinating and emerging through the soil. If the soil is too wet, damping off diseases may kill the crop. Slugs, snails and cutworms can damage or remove the entire crop if it is not protected (see page 168).

What's the right temperature for germination? Seed generally takes longer to germinate at low temperatures. For example, seed sown in early spring may take up to four weeks to germinate, whereas in the late spring, when the soil has warmed up, it will take only about two weeks.

In very early spring, when temperatures are low, it is pointless sowing seeds because they will merely sit in the soil, where they may come under attack from pests and diseases. I know we all start by reading the instructions on the packet, and if it states 'sow in early to mid-spring' that's when we think we must do it. However, if the soil is still too cold most seed will just rot or be very slow to germinate. More often than not, early sowing gives unsatisfactory results. For example, if you sow runner beans directly outside too early they will not grow, as the conditions are too cold and probably too wet.

In warmer areas, the soil will reach 10°C (50°F) a couple of weeks before the same type of soil in colder parts. If you live in a colder region and the recommended sowing date on the packet has passed, don't worry, because you will gain little by sowing before the soil temperature is right.

How deep should I sow the seeds? The correct sowing depth is important, and this information is stated on the seed packet. If the seeds are sown too deeply they will run out of food before they reach the soil surface. If sown too shallowly, the seeds may dry out because there are insufficient moisture supplies at the surface of the soil.

Generally speaking, small seeds contain little food so must not be put in too deep. Incorrect sowing depth is a common cause of failure.

To make a drill, place a broom or rake handle on the soil so that it is level with the soil surface. This gives a sufficient drill depth for most seed. Alternatively, you can mark a stick with centimetres or inches and use this as a guide when drawing it through the soil. Set out a plank or a line to keep the row straight if sowing in the ground. Sowing in a straight line makes it easy to identify the seeds when they come through the soil. Put a label at one end of the row so you know what the seedlings are later.

In practice, it is quite difficult to take out a drill to the right depth until you are experienced, but as you get more confident you can use the corner of a rake or a draw hoe to take out the drill.

When sowing into more than one drill, follow the spacing suggested on the packet or in the information about specific crops given in this book. Some crops are grown in double rows, where the rows will be sown closer together (see page 74).

Sowing the seeds

Seeds are usually sown continuously along the total length of the drill, and then thinned out later to the recommended spacing, or transplanted into another part of the plot.

Water the seeds in the drills before covering with soil and then water the seedbed lightly several times through a fine rose on the end of a watering can within the first hour of sowing. Covering the drills with clear polythene mulch after sowing will help to conserve moisture. Remove the sheet as soon as the seedlings come through the soil. Alternatively, cover the drills with cloches (see page 56).

Making a seed drill using a broom handle

Many seeds are dark in colour and very difficult to see when the soil is dark coloured. To help see their position and to get an idea of the number you have sown, sprinkle a bit of non-scented talcum powder into the seed packet before sowing, and shake the packet to mix the seeds with the talc. The seeds will then be covered lightly in talc and as this shows up clearly you can see what you have done.

Christine's tip

When watering a drill before seed sowing I use a watering can without a rose. Once there are seeds in the drill you need to use a can with a rose, to give a fine spray and avoid washing out the seeds.

Christine's tip

How many seeds should I sow? Sowing too many seeds is not only wasteful but will result in overcrowding. The seedlings will compete for water, light, air, nutrients and space, and their growth will be poor.

Nearly all seed packets tell you how many seeds they contain. Just look and think. For example, if a packet of parsnips contains 300 seeds and lettuce leaves 2,000 seeds, it is highly unlikely that you need to sow the whole packet at once. A pinch will be enough per 30cm (12in) of drill.

> If you only need a small amount of seed, split the packets with your gardening friends. If you still have a surplus, take it along to your horticultural or allotment society and pass it on to a good home.
>
> *Christine's tip*

Thinning and transplanting

Once the seeds have germinated they will start to grow and increase in size. When they are large enough to handle they can be thinned or transplanted to their final growing spacing. Always handle seedlings by the seed leaf, holding it between your finger and thumb.

The decision whether to sow and thin or sow and transplant is entirely personal, other than for root crops. These should not be transplanted as this can result in fanging and poor root development.

When seedlings are removed from a seedbed or from seed boxes for transplanting, up to 30 per cent of the root system can be torn off by the pulling action, causing a check to the seedlings' growth. There are several ways to avoid this transplanting check:

~ When sowing in a seedbed, incorporate plenty of compost to help promote a fibrous root system in friable soil.

~ Be sure to sow the seeds at the recommended rate. This gives the plants plenty of room to grow and helps prevent interweaving of roots, which makes lifting the plants out of the seedbed more difficult and will lead to root damage.

~ Do not allow your seedlings to get too big.

~ Water your seedlings a few hours before they are lifted and prise them out of the soil with care.

~ Transplant them on a dull day and water frequently until the young plants are established. This will help reduce the stress put on the plants by transpiration from the leaves.

~ Sow plants individually in containers.

In recent years there has been a trend towards growing plants in some form of container to start them off. These containers may be traditional plant pots, plastic cups, trays or old sandwich boxes which have divisions in them so that the plant is grown individually in its own space.

The major advantage of raising plants individually in containers is that it avoids a check when seedlings are transplanted. Once they are large enough to plant out they are then planted into the final positions with their roots intact in the original growing medium.

Sowing individual seeds into individual containers

Space or station sowing

You can use this method for large seeds such as peas, beans and parsnips, or for seed sold in tapes or pellets (see page 48).

Take out a drill to the recommended depth for the subject you wish to sow and place two or three seeds at the final crop spacing (or station), rather than sowing seeds along the total length of the drill. (See under each crop for spacing information.)

As some seeds may be eaten by slugs or fail to grow, sowing two or three per station means you should end up with at least one plant at the correct spacing. If all the seeds sown at a particular spacing germinate and escape attack, then thin them out to leave the strongest growing plant.

Sowing seed in a pot or container outside

The principles for sowing in a container are the same as for sowing in a seedbed. Fork or prick over the surface of the soil with a hand fork, remove any weeds, and then produce a tilth with the fork or use a rake if there is room.

Draw out a drill in a straight line and sow the seeds. Each drill should be a minimum of 15cm (6in) apart in a container.

Sowing for an early crop

You can produce many vegetables much earlier in the year than natural conditions usually allow and get greater yields if you raise them under some form of protection. The reasons for doing this are:

1. You can sow earlier and give the plants a longer growing season.
2. Temperatures are generally higher, which helps plants to grow more easily.
3. In their early stages of growth the plants are not exposed to the effects of the weather.

I start growing my half-hardy vegetables indoors in either late March or April. This means that, by the time they are planted out, the risk of having a hard frost that would kill them off is very small.

Forms of protection Three methods of protecting your plants and bringing them on early are:

~ pre-warming the soil in the seedbed with low polythene tunnels, frames or cloches before sowing

~ sowing in containers in a warm place such as a kitchen windowsill or in a heated greenhouse

~ sowing in heated propagating frames inside a cold greenhouse

A heated propagator may be used for seed raising

A low polythene tunnel warms the soil before seed sowing

Various cold frames made from wood, aluminium or plastic are available on the market and are great for growing plants in the early stages, and for hardening them off. I have eight in kit form, so I just put them together when I need them and then take them down and store them for next year. I do not have the space in my garden to keep them erected all year.

All my half-hardy seedlings are produced on my dining-room table or on the windowsills in the kitchen. I sow the seeds into seedtrays filled with seed and cutting compost, following the instructions on the packet for the depth of sowing. Once the seedlings are large enough to handle I move them into larger trays or pots, to give them more room. When most of the seedlings are about 8cm (3in) tall I then put them into a frame to harden them off (see below) before planting them outside once the danger of frost has passed.

How can I maximise the benefits from my frames and cloches? With early sowing, seedbed preparation will be much easier if the cloches or frames have been in place for a couple of weeks beforehand to warm up the soil and help it to dry out after the winter.

However, the soil should be adequately moist before sowing. Cloches help prevent moisture loss in sunny conditions, but you should check them every few days to ensure that there is enough moisture present. Condensation droplets on the leaves of plants can act as lenses, intensifying the sun's rays and causing burning, so take care to water the soil and not the foliage. Leave a small gap between individual cloches in the row to allow air to circulate.

During the winter, keep the cloches clean by washing them in soapy water. This will allow all the available light to reach the plants.

Hardening off If plants grown under any form of protection are planted straight into the garden they will be 'soft' and very prone to cold and frost damage. They will require hardening off to acclimatise them

to the cold conditions outside. This should be carried out over a 2–3 week period.

For plants raised in containers in a greenhouse or on a warm windowsill, move them into a frame outside for a few hours each day, gradually increasing the length of time. After a week, leave them in the frame or under the cloche and ventilate fully each day, by either opening the lid of the frame, raising the side of the cloche or opening its end walls.

You will need to ventilate plants growing in frames or under cloches more and more each day until the protection is completely removed. During very warm weather, it is best to take off the cloche ends to prevent the temperature under the cloche rising too high.

Remove the frame lid or the cloches completely during the daytime in the week in which you decide to finish using them, to allow the plants to harden off gradually, but replace them in the late afternoon. In early spring, outdoor temperatures can be quite high during the day, but fall quickly at night. This will help to minimise these temperature changes. Once the hardening-off process is complete, transfer the plants out into the ground.

Cloches and frames protect young seedlings

Mother Nature tells us all when to start seed sowing. Just watch your garden and as soon as the annual weeds are 6mm (¼in) tall it's time to start sowing your seeds. Wherever you are in the country, when the established weeds and the weed seedlings start into growth the soil is warm enough to receive the seeds you sow.

Christine's tip

Once you have sown all your crops and transplanted them to their final spacing, draw a diagram of your plot and mark on it the positions of all the crops and date it. In this way you will have a record to refer to next year so that you do not put the same crops in the same place year after year.

Christine's tip

chapter 5

WATERING

WATERING

Why do plants need water?

Plants need water to survive. It is the medium in which all the chemical processes in the plant take place.

Water is taken up by the plant through the roots; it passes up the stem and is given off at the leaf surface through tiny pores called stomata. Stomata are also present on the stems of all plants.

The opening and closing of these stomata controls the amount of water loss to the atmosphere. This loss is affected by many factors, such as the amount of sunshine, the relative humidity of the air, the temperature and the wind force (for example, a plant loses more water on a hot windy day than on a hot still day, because the wind dries the surface of the leaves). The size of the leaf, whether it is hairy or downy, and the waxiness of the leaf surface also affect the amount of water lost.

Large quantities of water pass through a plant during its life but only a small amount is used in the formation of tissue. The rest is used to keep the stomata open, which is vital for the plant's well-being, and to keep the plant's cells full of water (or turgid).

~ If the stomata close, the process of food manufacture (photosynthesis) stops.

~ Water loss through the leaves has a beneficial effect, cooling the plant.

~ If water is not available to the plant it wilts (the cells are said to be flaccid).

~ Water forms the solution of nutrients in the soil which are taken up by the plant and enable growth.

For all these reasons, water is vital for plant growth, but it is also important to apply the correct amount of water at the right time. If a plant has too much water while it is growing, plant nutrients are leached out of the soil and the plant will fail to develop a healthy root system, resulting in poor growth.

When some crops, such as peas and beans, are given too much water at the wrong stage of growth (see page 63), they may produce lush foliage at the expense of pod formation, and the edible part will not form.

How to water

What equipment do I need? You do not need a lot of equipment. I use a watering can without a rose to water the soil around plants or into open-bottomed flower pots, so that the water does not run away or off the surface on my very light soil. If I am watering a seed drill or seedbed I use a watering can with a very fine rose, to avoid disturbing the seeds, but I use a watering can without a rose when I need to water individual plants or the base of a seed drill to wet it before sowing seeds.

The only occasion that I use a hose, and then always with a spray head or gun attached, is when I need to give the whole vegetable plot a good soak. This is often following several weeks when rain has not fallen, which is common in my part of the country each summer. I never use a sprinkler.

How much water should I give? Always give plenty of water at one time, rather than little and often. It is better to apply 22 litres per sq m (4¾ gallons per sq yd) once a week than 5 litres per sq m (1 gallon per sq yd) three times a week.

The soil wets in layers. Until the surface is wet, the layer beneath will remain dry. Watering lightly on the surface is basically a waste of time because the water does not penetrate the first layer and the soil below remains dry. Repeated light watering can, in fact, promote surface rooting, which makes the plant more prone to wilting in dry conditions as its roots are unable to search deeply for water.

What time of day is best for watering? Always try to water first thing in the morning or last thing in the evening, rather than in the middle of the day when the temperature is at its highest. This helps to prevent excessive evaporation.

Some people say not to water at night as dampness in the foliage may encourage disease. In practice I have not found this to be a problem provided that the water is directed to the base of the plant.

Watering to establish seeds and seedlings

All plants require water when germinating and during the period in which they are becoming established.

Water is vital for the process of germination; if you sow into soil that is dry, the seed cannot absorb water and germination does not take place. So if your soil is not moist at the time of sowing, water the bottom of the seed drill before sowing the seed, and keep the soil moist until the seeds have germinated.

Watering at transplanting

When any plant is transplanted there is generally some damage to the root system, which affects water uptake after transplanting. Normally a plant's leaf area is larger than the root area and, if the plant is placed in dry soil and not watered in, the leaves give out water quicker than the roots can take it in and the plant wilts. The plant's stomata close and this reduces the growth rate, and can also affect final yield.

Research has shown that container-raised plants get away to a much better start if they have been watered before and after transplanting. For any plant, whether it is growing in a seedbed or in a container, make sure you have watered it at least 24 hours before transplanting and then again after, to ensure that both the root ball and the soil into which the new roots are to grow are moist.

Once planted, keep the seedlings well watered. In dry weather you should apply about 150ml (5fl oz) of water daily at the base of each plant, until it is established and starts growing rapidly.

Watering during growth

Some plants (such as leafy vegetables) respond to water throughout their lives, while others (for example, peas) only respond at critical times during their growth. This reaction stage is called the critical period.

You can adjust your watering depending on the crop being grown, as some don't need watering outside their critical periods. Bearing in mind that water is an important resource which we will all end up paying for through a metering system, it must be a good idea to water sensibly rather than wasting water on plants that won't benefit from it.

Leafy vegetables These include brassicas, celery, lettuce and spinach. To produce tender leafy vegetables, their growth must not be checked at any time due to lack of water or nutrients.

Generally speaking, most leafy vegetables should receive 11 litres of water per sq m (2½ gallons per sq yd) each week during the summer. If you are unable to do this because your water supply is restricted, just water the plants at sowing and at transplanting until they are established, and then leave them to fend for themselves until about 3–4 weeks before you expect to harvest them. Then apply 22 litres per sq m (4¾ gallons per sq yd). This will result in an increase in plant growth during the last two weeks of maturing.

Brussels sprouts are the exception in this group. They should be watered after planting and until established but then, because they are widely spaced, they should not be watered again.

Cauliflower A check to growth due to water shortage at an early stage may result in 'buttoning', when very small curds are produced early in the season.

Celery Daily watering is beneficial under dry conditions as it prevents the stalks becoming very stringy or pithy, making them unpleasant to eat.

Lettuce and spinach If these are short of water they will wilt and stop growing.

Root vegetables and tubers If you apply too much water to beetroot, carrots, parsnips or radishes, for example, they will produce lush foliage with little root growth. Your aim should be to provide a constant supply of water to maintain even growth.

During the early stages apply 5 litres per sq m (1 gallon per sq yd), but once they are growing well give 22 litres per sq m (4¾ gallons per sq yd) once every two weeks, if needed. Try to keep the soil moist; if you let it dry out before watering or if it rains very heavily, the roots may split.

Potatoes Watering depends on what you are trying to achieve and what varieties you are growing.

~ For a high yield of early potatoes, water throughout the growing period at two-week intervals, with 22 litres per sq m (4¾ gallons per sq yd) on each occasion.

~ If earliness is what matters, do not provide water until the tuber is at the marble stage, which is normally at flowering. Then give one application of 22 litres per sq m (4¾ gallons per sq yd).

~ With maincrop potatoes, do not apply water until the tubers start forming, which is normally at the start of flowering. Then a single application of 27 litres per sq m (6 gallons per sq yd) of water can produce good results.

Some varieties will tolerate dry conditions better than others. For example, 'Home Guard', 'Arran Pilot', 'Pentland Crown' and 'Vanessa' seem to cope in dry seasons.

Fruiting vegetables These are crops where the fruit is eaten; for example, beans and peas, cucumbers, marrows and tomatoes.

Beans and peas Water at flowering time and when the fruits are swelling. Once germination has occurred and the young plants are through the soil, do not water until flowering starts (unless severe wilting takes place). Watering throughout the plant's life encourages the growth of lots of stem and leaf at the expense of the crop.

Once flowering occurs, water the plants twice a week with 11 litres per sq m (2½ gallons per sq yd) and continue as the pods swell. Direct the water at the base of the plants. Research has shown that keeping the root zone of runner beans moist will increase the number of beans which set, and this practice will also prevent peas and beans getting tough.

Cucumbers, marrows and courgettes Apply water freely throughout the life of the plant to ensure rapid growth and fruit development, especially once the fruit starts to develop. It is a good idea to direct the water to the base of the plant and not all over the soil surface. This saves water (because you are reducing the area over which rapid evaporation will take place) and it also helps prevent the fruits being splashed with mud, which can result in rotting.

When watering members of the marrow family, try
not to wet the foliage of the plant and do not splash
water all over the soil. Place your thumb over the
end of the spout to control the flow.

Christine's tip

Tomatoes For tomatoes grown outside in the ground, water until they are established and then stop until they begin to flower. This will encourage the roots to grow down into the soil. When flowers appear, apply 22 litres of water per sq m (4¾ gallons per sq yd) every week. If plants are short of water at this stage, small fruits will form and you will get a small yield.

Whether grown under cover or outside, tomatoes in grow bags or in compost in containers will need to be watered throughout their life because, unlike plants growing in the ground, they do not have an area for the roots to explore. Do not allow the plants to dry out or problems such as split fruit, blossom end rot and poor growth may occur.

Ways to reduce watering

Adding organic matter Regular applications of any type of bulky organic matter will improve the water-holding capacity of your soil, with the effect that more water will be available to your plants.

Adding organic matter improves the structure of the soil and this in turn helps root growth and penetration. The plants can produce roots that will explore a larger area of soil, giving them the chance to extract more water. When plants can absorb water from a large area you do not have to water as often as when they have small, shallow-growing roots.

Deep digging Double digging (see page 23) your vegetable garden every three years will help to break up the soil, making it more open and easier for roots to penetrate.

Weeding Weeds compete with plants for water as well as for light and nutrients. If you allow lots of weeds to grow and develop, your plants will not get all the available water, nutrients and light they could be getting, and this will affect crop growth and yields.

Established weeds utilise large amounts of water and it is best to remove all the weeds when they are small (see page 162). This aids moisture conservation and also helps to keep plants healthy, as some weeds can harbour pests and diseases.

Sparse or wide planting If you space your plants more widely than normal, each plant has a larger area and volume of soil from which it can draw water without competition. This is a useful technique on soils which are very light and free draining, and can easily be adopted if you have lots of spare ground.

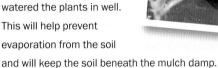

Mulching Cover the soil surface with a layer of organic or inorganic material after planting, having first watered the plants in well. This will help prevent evaporation from the soil and will keep the soil beneath the mulch damp.

Providing shelter Reducing the wind speed in your garden by providing some sort of shelter will help to lessen water loss from the soil by evaporation, but do not forget that living windbreaks compete for water with your crops. If you have a windbreak or a row of plants which give shelter, mulch these heavily to help retain moisture, and water freely when you have water to spare.

Cultivating shallowly During dry conditions, try not to bring any moist soil to the surface when you are working because this will cause the soil to dry out very quickly. Limit your cultivations to surface hoeing, to remove weeds.

Hoeing creates 'dust' mulch which breaks down the network of channels through which water passes to the surface and is lost by evaporation. Hoe through the crop once a week to keep the weeds down and also to conserve water.

chapter 6

·LEGUMES

What are legumes? 'Legume' is the collective name for the seeds of the pea family (*Leguminosae*) which includes the culinary peas and broad, runner and French beans. Members of the legume family are particularly sensitive to moisture stress so should be grown in moisture-retentive soils. If your soil is quick to drain and does not hold water for long, you will improve the water-holding capacity by incorporating plenty of organic matter and make growing peas and beans much easier. Members of this family have been shown to have critical periods when water should be given to obtain the best results (see page 63).

If you look at the roots of legumes you will find little swellings on them known as root nodules. These are formed by bacteria which are essential to the health of the plant and also for maintaining general soil fertility by fixing atmospheric nitrogen. The nodules convert the atmospheric nitrogen into an organic form which is made available to the plant. For this reason nitrogen is not generally given in the base dressing for peas and beans.

Peas

Peas are generally grown for the seeds inside the pod, but sometimes the pods are picked while the peas are quite small and the whole pod cooked just like French beans. These peas are called mangetout. By careful selection of different varieties and by sowing on different dates (successional sowing), fresh peas can be available from early summer to early autumn.

'Half Pint'

'Feltham First'

'Kelvedon Wonder'

'Oregon Sugar Pod'

Which variety should I grow?

If you are unsure which variety to grow ask a gardening friend or a member of your gardening or allotment club, but over the years I have grown the following varieties with great success:

In containers
'Junos', 'Lincoln' and 'Half Pint' – low growing and generally do not need support

In the ground
'Feltham First', 'Hurst Green Shaft', 'Kelvedon Wonder' and 'Misty'

Mangetout
'Delikata' and 'Oregon Sugar Pod'

Sowing your crop

The traditional method of sowing peas states that a flat-bottomed drill should be used. I have never really found out why this is recommended and for the beginner it's one of the most difficult types of drill to produce. Over the years I have found that it is not necessary and have produced very successful crops by doing the following:

Prepare the seedbed (see page 49) but do not apply any nitrogen in the base dressing as it is not necessary. Stretch a garden line tightly between two pegs at the ends of the row to make a straight line and then use an old, thin broom handle to make a 5cm (2in) deep hole every 12cm (5in) along the line. Pop two seeds in each hole. Move the line 15cm (6in) from the first row and repeat the exercise to make a double row of peas (see page 74). If you want to grow more than one double row, the distance between the double rows should be the expected height of the crop. This information is often given on the seed packet. After sowing the seeds, fill the holes with soil and water well.

An alternative way of growing peas, and one which is very popular, is to get some roof guttering, fill it with good compost and sow the peas in the gutter, placing one seed every 12cm (5in) along the guttering. For a double row you will need two pieces of guttering. Once the peas are about 8cm (3in) tall, make a depression in the prepared soil in the ground and slide the peas out of the gutter into their new spot without disturbing them.

Growing your crop

When the peas are about 10cm (4in) tall they will start to produce their first tendrils and will need some form of support. If the plant has nothing to climb up it will flop to the ground where slugs will cause considerable damage.

Sow *direct*	mid-March–July
Harvest	June–October

For support I use pea sticks, which in reality are dead, woody shrub prunings which I keep and dry every year. They are twiggy and are great not only for supporting the crop but also for helping to keep the birds away. Birds, especially pigeons, can do a lot of damage by picking off the top of the plant, or even pulling the seedling up completely. Some people suggest using pea netting to support the crop. Yes, it works, but at the end of the season it takes for ever to unwind all the growth from the netting. I never have the patience for this job and in the past have thrown the netting away as it was taking far too long.

Once supported there is not a lot to be done. Do not water too often or you will get plants that produce lots of healthy leaves which grow really well but no flowers. I have found it's best not to water them at all after they are established and then to start again once they come into flower (see page 64).

When the seeds have come through the ground, mulching the ground between the rows with compost, paper or grass clippings will help conserve water as well as keep the weeds down. Never use grass clippings from a lawn which has been treated with weedkiller.

Peas can also be grown in containers such as old baths or old fish boxes. I find a minimum depth of 30cm (12in) is needed to provide enough water when the crop is in flower. Make sure the container has drainage holes as peas rot very quickly if the roots are surrounded by water. Do not sow in rows but plant the whole surface up by sowing the seeds 12cm (5in) apart. I tend to do this in circles around the edge of the pot and work towards the centre, but it does not really matter provided you do not put them too close together. Once the seedlings are 10cm (4in) high, stake them with pea sticks, and then treat them like normal peas (see above).

The dwarf types are great in window boxes and even in hanging baskets, so just use your imagination and enjoy a few pickings of home-grown peas – there's nothing like them fresh from the pod with a bit of mint and butter!

Particular problems to watch out for

Pea moth

The major pest of peas is *pea moth*. Look out for small caterpillars up to 6mm (¼in) long with greenish-yellow bodies and black heads. They feed on peas by burrowing through the pod and into the individual peas, making them inedible.

Damage is worst in mid- and late summer. Bad attacks can be prevented by sowing early or late, not during early or mid-spring, to avoid the plants being in flower during early and mid-summer. If you do sow in the first part of spring, cover the row with horticultural fleece at the beginning of summer to prevent the moth from laying its eggs on the plant.

Harvesting and storage

Regular picking will encourage flowering and so more peas will form. Pick the pods when the peas still have some room to swell. Do not let them get any bigger or they will lose their sweetness. Pick mangetout when the tiny peas inside the pod are just visible and starting to swell.

The best way to store peas is to freeze them. Pick only unblemished peas for storing.

Do not allow the pods to remain on the plants once swollen. If you do they will start developing into seed and this will reduce the numbers of flowers produced and hence the crop.

Once you have finally harvested all your crop, cut off the foliage at ground level and put it on the compost heap. Do not pull up the roots. Dig the roots in during the autumn to provide nitrogen for the next crop that occupies the soil.

Christine's tips

To attract beneficial insects which help to pollinate legumes I grow sweet peas up against all my fences surrounding the vegetable garden. This looks nice and provides me with lots of cut flowers but it also attracts insects. Another thing you can do is to grow herbs inside gumboots and just stand these among your vegetables or hang them from a fence or shed. When in flower they will attract a lot of insects.

Christine's tip

Broad beans

These are one of the easiest legumes to grow and can look great when grown among flowers in borders and beds, so don't just sow them in the vegetable garden – mix them in the flower garden as well.

They produce very attractive white and black-coloured flowers, followed by the productive pods which can be eaten when only 8cm (3in) long or you can allow the beans to swell and pick the pods when the beans have swollen.

Sowing your crop

Seed is generally sown outdoors in a double row, in drills 5cm (2in) deep. Sow the seeds of dwarf varieties 23cm (9in) apart in rows that are also 23cm (9in) apart. For tall varieties allow 45cm (18in) between the rows and 23cm (9in) between the seeds in the row.

If you have a greenhouse or a kitchen windowsill you can start your beans off early by sowing one seed per 10cm (4in) pot in mid-winter to have young plants ready for hardening off and planting out in early to mid-spring, once 8cm (3in) high. Harvest from the beginning of summer onwards.

If growing them among flowers either sow in situ allowing 20cm (8in) between the beans or other plants in early or mid-spring, or sow them individually in 10cm (4in) pots and then plant them out when you plant your flowering plants or when they are about 10cm (4in) high.

They also grow really well in containers with a minimum 30cm (12in) depth of soil. Sow as I have described above for peas in containers but space the seed 20cm (8in) apart. They can look great when sown directly in deep window boxes, especially in two rows if space allows. I have also seen them growing well in deep washing-up bowls.

You can also sow broad beans from mid- to late autumn. These plants will give you a crop about 2–3 weeks earlier than from a spring sowing. The standard variety used for an autumn sowing is 'Aquadulce Claudia'. It is very hardy and produces a very early crop. It does not need protection at all and is a white-seeded variety.

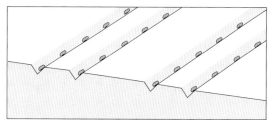
Double rows

Which variety should I grow?

'Bunyards Exhibition'

'Imperial Green Longpod'

'The Sutton'

In open ground

Two colours of seed can be grown: white seeded or green. Both are delicious when served with new potatoes and gammon or bacon. My favourites include:

'Bunyards Exhibition' – white seeded
'Green Windsor' – green seeded
'Imperial Green Longpod' – green seeded
'Imperial White Longpod' – white seeded

In containers

'The Sutton' – dwarf, white seeded

Sow *under cover*	February
Sow *direct*	March–May
	late October–November
Harvest	May–July

After harvesting cut off the foliage if it is not diseased and put it on the compost heap. Dig the roots into the soil as, like those of peas, they contain nitrogen. In the flower border, just cut off the plants at ground level and allow the roots to disintegrate in situ.

Christine's tip

Growing your crop

Once the plants are about 10cm (4in) tall, erect a support system. I use canes and then just put strong twine around the canes in the rows to support tall varieties. If you are growing them in the flower garden, stake the tall varieties individually with a cane and tie the plant to the cane with twine. Dwarf varieties generally do not need to be staked.

To reduce competition from weeds hoe regularly and apply a mulch to conserve water (see page 64 for watering).

When the plants have formed four or five clusters of pods, remove the top 10cm (4in) of growth from the plants. This helps to provide some control over blackfly (see below) and encourages the pods to swell, which helps to ensure an early harvest.

Particular problems to watch out for

The major pest of broad beans is the *black bean aphid*. Large colonies of blackfly appear on the shoot tips at the end of spring through the summer. They stunt growth, damage the flowers and cause the pods to be distorted. To prevent severe attacks, pinch out the top growth as described above.

If you wish to spray, use an insecticide recommended for this crop. Do not spray when the plants are in full flower as you may kill the bees and other beneficial insects which help pollinate the crop.

The major disease to look out for is *chocolate spot*. This disease appears as small brown spots on the leaves and occasionally as dark streaks on the stem. In severe attacks the spots may join together

Removing the growing point from broad beans

and kill the plant. You can help prevent this disease by not growing the plants too close together – so don't reduce the spacing suggested – and by growing your plants strongly. To do this, use a base dressing at sowing (but do not apply any nitrogen), and then apply a top dressing of potash fertiliser about six weeks after germination, following the instructions on the packet.

Harvesting and storage

You can harvest broad beans for their immature pods when they are about 8cm (3in) long. Cooked whole and served with a white sauce they are delicious. Otherwise start picking as soon as the beans start to show through the pod.

To check that you are picking at the correct time, open up one of the pods and remove the beans. If the scar left by removal from the pod is white the crop should be tender but if it is black the beans have gone past their best.

Beans can be easily frozen but only unblemished beans should be selected.

Black bean aphid   Chocolate spot

Runner beans

Runner beans are grown mainly for immature, long, flat-podded fruits. They are generally grown as climbing plants and are particularly susceptible to wind damage, which you can prevent by providing shelter (see page 12).

Dwarf varieties are now available for growing in containers such as hanging baskets and window boxes or for growing among flowers. In both cases allow 20cm (8in) between each plant.

For maximum success incorporate lots of organic matter into the soil as this helps to retain moisture and satisfies the bean's requirement for a well-structured, moisture-retentive soil.

Sow *under cover*	March–May
Sow *direct*	late May–July
Harvest	June–October

Which variety should I grow?

In the vegetable garden or in a flower border up a wigwam, or against a fence, trellis panel or wall, try any of these climbing types:

'Celebration' – salmon pink flowers
'Painted Lady' – a lovely bean with striking red and white flowers; looks great in among flowers or shrubs
'Painted Lady' and 'St George' – red and white flowers
'Red Rum' – red flowers
'Summer Medley' – a delightful mix of red, white and pink flowers
'White Swan' – white flowers

In containers or among other plants:
'Hestia' – dwarf variety reaching 30–45cm (12–18in) high; red and white flowers; producing 20cm (8in) long pods

'Celebration'

'Painted Lady'

'Red Rum'

'Summer Medley'

'White Swan'

'Hestia'

Sowing your crop

In practice, runners always surprise you and it has taken me years to learn not to sow too many seeds, resulting in being swamped by them when they start cropping.

I have found that sowing 10 seeds into individual 10cm (4in) pots, on my dining-room table or kitchen windowsill, in mid-spring, and then planting the strongest five plants up a wigwam, when all risk of frost has passed, provides plenty for one person. I erect the wigwam so that the canes are 30cm (12in) apart.

In early summer I then sow another 10 seeds into pots and when big enough I transplant the strongest five plants to the base of the original wigwam and let them climb up the older plants. In this way I have a continuity of beans from early summer through to mid-autumn.

Traditionally plants are grown outside in situ and to do this they require warm growing conditions. The seed will not germinate unless the soil temperature is above 12°C (53°F). Therefore, on most soils do not sow until late spring when the soil temperature will be sufficiently warm.

Put down a garden line and make holes 5cm (2in) deep and 30cm (12in) apart, sowing two seeds per hole. Move the line 40cm (15in) away from the first row and repeat the exercise. Once the plants have germinated, remove the weakest seedling to leave one plant per station.

If you do want to get an early start, sow some seeds in a warm greenhouse or kitchen windowsill singly into 10cm (4in) pots, but do not plant them out until the risk of frost has passed, or you will lose your plants through frost damage.

Growing your crop

Once your plants are 10cm (4in) tall, erect a support system for them. If growing by the traditional method, insert one cane beside each plant and then tie the opposite cane together at the top. Placing a cane along the top of these tied canes and tying them altogether will add stability (see diagram below). Alternatively, just grow them up a wigwam.

To keep down weeds you should hoe regularly and to help conserve moisture mulch the crop with organic matter (see page 64 for watering). Once the plants get to the top of the support, nip out the growing point. This is known as stopping or pinching.

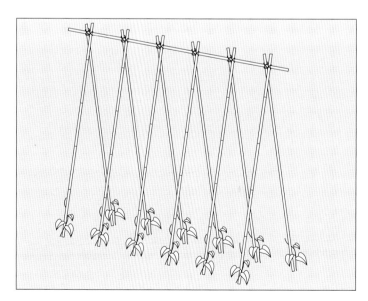
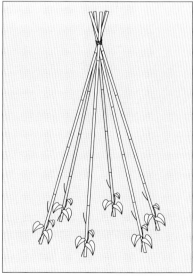

Traditional methods of supporting runner beans

Particular problems to watch out for

A problem to look out for is the *absence of flowers or pods* and there are several reasons for this occurring. One is an over-application of fertiliser and another is applying too much water at the wrong time, which results in lush leaves and good foliage growth but few, if any, flowers being produced.

Very cold or windy weather can prevent insects such as bees from pollinating the crop. Flowers will appear but no pods will set.

If the season is very hot and dry it is essential to keep the roots moist and applying mulch will help to conserve moisture. It is equally important to water at the correct stage with the right amount (see page 64).

Halo blight   Anthracnose

It was said in the past that spraying the flowers with water helped them set. Work carried out several years ago at a research institute showed this to have little effect, but what was found to be important was the moisture at the roots. New research indicates that water application to the roots in the evening increases cropping and pod set.

The disease *halo blight* may be a problem on both runner and French beans. Small brown spots surrounded with a yellow 'halo' are produced on the leaves, while the pods develop water-soaked spots. Halo blight is always worst in a wet season. Prevent problems by never soaking the seeds before sowing and use a resistant variety such as 'Red Rum'.

If brown sunken spots which with time turn pink appear on the pods, the plant is suffering from the disease *anthracnose*. Grow a resistant variety such as 'Kelvedon Stringless' and carry out crop rotation.

Harvesting and storage

Pick regularly to ensure further flowering and pod formation and to prevent the pods becoming stringy. If you have too many to use fresh they can be frozen, salted or even dried.

French beans

French or kidney beans are grown mainly for the pods, which are eaten when immature. They can be dried and stored for winter use. Like runner beans, French beans need warm soil to encourage germination and good growth. Do not sow until the soil temperature is at least 10°C (50°F), which is likely to be in mid- or late spring depending on

where you live. If you want to get some plants off to an early start, sow seeds in 10cm (4in) pots in a heated greenhouse in early spring. They can also be started off on your kitchen windowsill.

Sowing your crop

Dwarf types look great growing in containers or in the flower border. If grown in this manner, sow the seeds 15cm (6in) apart and 5cm (2in) deep. They do not require any support.

When sowing the seeds traditionally, sow in 5cm (2in) deep drills, allowing 60cm (24in) between rows and 23cm (9in) between seeds in the row. Sow two seeds at each station and thin the weaker seedling after germination. Climbing types should be staked as suggested for runner beans on page 78.

Growing your crop

French beans have the same cultural requirements as runners so should be grown in the same way (see page 78).

Particular problems to watch out for

These beans suffer the same problems as runner beans (see page 79).

Harvesting and storage

Pick regularly when the pods are 10–20cm (4–8in) long. The pods should snap easily when you bend them.

French beans can be frozen or dried (haricots). If you want dried beans, let the plants turn brown and then pull them up and hang them somewhere dry. When the pods are brittle, shell the seeds and store them in a closed container.

'Purple Teepee'

'The Prince'

'Valdor Golden'

'Cobra'

Which variety should I grow?

Green and coloured varieties are available, as are bush types and climbing types. The pods may be flat or pencil-like.

Dwarf French beans

'Ferrari' – pencil podded, green
'Maxi Organic' – pencil podded, green
'Purple Teepee' – round podded, purple
'The Prince' – flat podded, green
'Valdor Golden' – round podded, yellow

Climbing beans

'Algarve' – flat podded, mid-green
'Cobra' – round podded, green

Sow *under cover*	March–May
Sow *direct*	late May–July
Harvest	June–October

If you are going to be away from home for a period of time and there is no one to harvest your peas or beans, then remove all the flowers just before you go away. This will encourage the plant to produce far more flowers at a slightly later date, hopefully once you are back home to enjoy the crop.

If the pods are not picked they will start to form seed and this will prevent more flowers being produced.

Christine's tip

chapter 7

ONIONS

and related crops

Which vegetables belong to the onion family? Onions, shallots, garlic and leeks all belong to the onion family (*Alliaceae*) and are grown for their bulbs, leaves and small bulbs where salad or spring onions are concerned, or the white shanks (stems) in the case of leeks.

With all members of the onion family, crop rotation is important. It minimises soil-borne pest and disease problems which can make growing the crop impossible.

Bulb onions

There are two types of onion, one which is globe shaped and the other flat bottomed. Breeding has resulted in European types and Japanese types, which means that you can now have onions for use all the year round. As Japanese types mature earlier in the year than European types, they fill the gap before the latter are ready for harvesting.

Bulb onions may be grown either from seed or from sets, which are immature onion bulbs. If you have never grown onions before or you have grown them from seed but were disappointed, try growing them from sets, which is not as demanding as growing onions from seed.

It is the length of daylight that makes onions start to form a bulb. The European types which are sown in early spring will start to bulb from late spring when the days are 16 hours long, while the Japanese types which are sown in the late summer start to bulb from early spring when days are 12 hours long.

The ultimate size of the bulb is determined by the number of leaves the plant has produced by the time it starts to form a bulb.

Sowing your crop

The seed may be sown in modules or seedtrays under heated protection in mid-winter and then pricked out and grown on in containers – pots or modules – until planting out in early spring after being hardened off.

If sowing outdoors in situ prepare the soil (see page 49) and then take out a drill 1cm (½in) deep. Any time from early spring sow the seeds thinly along its length, cover with soil and water well.

Thin in stages, using the thinnings as salad onions. The ultimate size of the onion is determined by spacing. For medium-sized onions space 15cm (6in) apart each way. For larger bulbs space 18cm (7in) apart each way.

'Bedfordshire Champion'

'Red Baron'

'Senshyu Yellow'

'F1 Hytech'

Which variety should I grow?

Bulb onions from seed
'Bedfordshire Champion' – globe shaped
'Red Baron' – globe shaped
'Cipollini Yellow' – flat bottomed

Japanese overwintering types
'Keepwell' F1 – slightly flattened round bulbs
'Senshyu Yellow' – semi-globe shaped

Bulb onions from sets
'F1 Hyred' – red skinned, pink flesh
'F1 Hytech' – semi-globe with good storage ability

Sow *under cover*	January–March
Plant *out*	late March–April
Sow *direct*	March–July
Plant *sets*	February–March
Harvest	
Japanese	June–July
European	mid-July–August

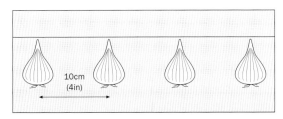

Plant onion sets with their necks just below the surface

Growing your crop

In my experience it is best to grow onions from seed in the vegetable garden but from sets in flower borders.

When growing from sets, prepare the seedbed as described on page 49. The soil does not need to be as fine as for seed. Put down a garden line and then plant the bulbs (sets) 10cm (4in) apart in the row and allow 23cm (9in) between the rows.

The sets should be planted with the tip just below the soil surface. Some people believe the tip should be showing, but I have found that if you do this the birds will pull out the sets. I have found no detrimental effect in planting with the tip just under the soil (see diagram above). Avoid pushing the sets into the soil as this will compact the soil beneath and when the roots start to grow they will push the set out of the soil. Use a trowel to plant the sets. Firm the soil around each one after planting.

Either seed or sets can be grown in containers. Providing a minimum soil depth of 15cm (6in) is available, good results can be obtained by growing onions in such containers as washing-up bowls, as long as they have drainage holes (see page 32). Window boxes are also useful and they make a very ornamental feature when planted up with trailing plants over the edge. However, don't go overboard with the ornamentals as they will grow and cover the developing bulb, creating too much competition and making ripening difficult, so just use trailing plants and do not plant the top of the window box.

Onions are very susceptible to weed competition in the first six weeks after sowing, so ensure regular weeding takes place in the early stages.

Irrigation is not normally needed except in very dry seasons, but water should never be given after mid-summer as this will delay maturity and impair storage quality.

Particular problems to watch out for

White rot

White rot will cause the leaves to turn yellow and the plant to wilt. A white fluffy mould grows at the base of the plant, often with round black bits (fungal bodies) appearing in the white fungus. The disease is worst in dry summers. There is no treatment so remove all diseased plants and destroy, and do not grow onions for at least eight years. It may also occur on shallots and spring onions.

Bolting means that the plant has prematurely run to flower. It may happen due to an incorrect planting date, planting in too cold a soil or loose planting. When this occurs, cut off the flower stalk and do not store the bulb.

Rust may also be a problem (see page 91).

Harvesting and storage

European onions are ready for harvesting by the end of the summer when the leaves will have bent over naturally. Japanese types will be ready in early summer.

Once the majority of the crop has fallen over, take a fork and lift the bulbs from the soil. If the weather is good leave the bulbs on the soil surface to dry out completely and become straw coloured.

Store the onions in nets in a well-ventilated, frost-free place. Only store those bulbs which are free from damage or disease.

spring onions

Spring onions or salad onions are small, white-skinned onions grown primarily for the use of their white shanks and green leaves in salads. You can have a supply for nearly every month of the year if you use different sowing dates and varieties.

Sowing your crop

Prepare the seedbed and drills (see page 49). Make a 1cm (½in) deep drill and sow the seeds thinly along rows 10cm (4in) apart.

Growing your crop

Once the seedlings are through the soil keep them weeded to help reduce competition. Apply water during the growing season at a rate of 11 litres per sq m (2½ gallons per sq yd) as often as necessary to maintain growth. If you are going to transplant them into containers, hanging baskets or window boxes, allow the seedlings to grow to 8cm (3in) tall before lifting them and planting into their new position.

Due to the upright nature of their growth they are ideal for growing in window boxes, containers and even in hanging baskets. If you obtain a window box that is at least 20cm (8in) wide you can grow a row of salad onions, a row of radishes and a row of salad leaves all together on your windowsill. Once you have harvested all the crops, re-sow it and start again. After a year replace the soil with new soil. A John Innes No.2 will be fine or use your garden soil.

Particular problems to watch out for

White rot may be a problem (see page 85).

Harvesting

Gently pull the young plants out of the soil when the bulb is about 1–2cm (½–¾in) in diameter. Salad onions are not suitable for storage and are best eaten soon after harvesting.

'Shimonita'

'White Lisbon'

Which variety should I grow?

'Shimonita' – a winter-hardy Japanese salad onion
'White Lisbon' – the traditional 'spring' onion; sow from early spring to early autumn
'White Lisbon Winter Hardy' – suitable for autumn sowing and a spring harvest
'White Sear' F_1 – repeat sowings for a continuous supply

Sow *direct*	March–September
Harvest	nearly every month

You will find it much easier to lift spring onions if you water the rows a couple of hours before harvesting.

Christine's tip

Shallots

Shallots are bulbs which are fully grown when you buy them. They start to grow when you plant them out in spring and by the end of the season have produced a cluster of 8–10 similar-sized bulbs to the ones you planted. They are generally used for pickling or for cooking but may be eaten raw. Both yellow and red varieties are available.

Planting your crop

Shallots require a long growing season and should be planted as soon as the soil is workable, usually in late spring. If you are one of the lucky gardeners who has very well-drained soil you can plant them slightly earlier.

Prepare the seedbed (see page 49) and then take out a drill about 5cm (2in) deep. The ultimate size of the bulb is dependent upon the amount of growing room it is given. For reasonably sized shallots space the rows 20cm (8in) apart and allow 15cm (6in) between each set, but for large ones allow 30cm (12in) between the rows and 15cm (6in) between the sets. Put the shallot into the base of the drill and cover with soil so that the neck is just below the surface (see page 85). If you plant with the neck showing birds tend to pull them out of the ground, but planting them so all of the neck is buried prevents this.

If growing in a container such as a window box, space the sets so that there is 20cm (8in) between them in each direction. Just as with onions, do not grow other crops alongside shallots when growing them in containers as it restricts bulb development.

Growing your crop

If frost occurs after planting, go out into your garden and check that the shallots have not been lifted out of the ground. If they have, replant them. Once the shoots have come through the soil, grow the shallots as you would onions (see page 85).

'Golden Gourmet'   'Yellow Moon'

Which variety should I grow?

'Golden Gourmet'

'Red Gourmet'

'Yellow Moon'

| **Plant** *sets* | February–March |
| **Harvest** | June–July |

Particular problems to watch out for

White rot may be a problem (see page 85).

Harvesting and storage

During early or mid-summer the leaves will start to turn brown. Lift the shallots and split each cluster into separate bulbs. Put them somewhere to dry out thoroughly. Once they are dry, break off the dried stems and store the bulbs in nets as you would for onions or make into a rope. They store more reliably than any other onion and should keep for about 8–9 months.

Do not be tempted to buy very small shallots as they are unlikely to give you a satisfactory crop. Ideally each set should be about 15–20g (3/4oz).

Christine's tip

Leeks

Leeks are grown for the white area at the base of the stem known as the shank, and are generally harvested from early autumn through to early spring.

Sowing your crop

Leeks are generally sown from seeds in a seedbed in early or mid-spring and are then planted out from late spring to mid-summer. Prepare your seedbed (see page 49) and make drills 1–2cm (½ – ¾in) deep and 30cm (12in) apart. Sow your leeks thinly, aiming at about 40 seeds per metre (yard) of drill.

'King Richard'   'Musselburgh'

Which variety should I grow?

'Carlton' and 'Electra' – early varieties, harvesting from early autumn to early winter; suitable for growing in a container or pulling as a salad onion

'King Richard' – an early variety, ready from early autumn to early winter; less powerful flavour than some spring onion varieties; suitable for growing in a container or pulling as a salad onion

'Lyon-Prizetaker' – early variety, harvesting from early autumn to early winter

'Musselburgh' – harvesting from early to late winter

'Giant Winter' – harvesting from late winter to mid-spring

Sow *outside*	March–April
Harvest	September–March

Planting your crop

Your leeks will be ready for transplanting when they are about 20cm (8in) tall, approximately 12 weeks after sowing. The main transplanting season is from late spring through to mid-summer. Water the row well a few hours before you are due to lift and transplant the leeks, as this will lessen damage to the plants.

Prepare the area for planting by raking 25g per sq m (1oz per sq yd) of sulphate of ammonia into the soil. Leeks require high levels of nitrogen at planting time (which this fertiliser will provide), but in the late summer be careful not to apply excess nitrogen as this will encourage sappy growth which reduces winter hardiness.

Planting is quite easy. Put a garden line in place where you want your leeks to grow. Make holes 15cm (6in) deep in rows 30cm (12in) apart with 15cm (6in) between the holes. Lift your plants and trim a small amount off both the leaves and roots and then just drop one leek plant into each hole. Do not fill the hole with soil, just water the plants in well.

Growing your crop

Hoe the soil regularly to get rid of weeds, thereby reducing competition. Supply plenty of water (22 litres per sq m/4¾ gallons per sq yd) only during dry, warm weather to help the leeks produce good shanks.

If you want long, white shanks 'blanching' will be necessary. Excluding light from the leek stems prevents the formation of chlorophyll (the pigment in plants which makes them look green). White tissue is produced instead. You can do this simply by drawing dry soil up around the stems of the leeks with a draw hoe.

During the summer, just before earthing up, mix 20g per sq m (¾oz per sq yd) of the fertiliser Growmore into the soil. This will ensure that the leeks are able to produce good growth rapidly.

Particular problems to watch out for

Rust is a disease which causes orange spots to appear on the surface of the leaves which with time become powdery. The leaves may turn yellow and die. Overcome the

Rust

problem by growing rust-resistant varieties such as 'Autumn Giant 2 Porvite', 'Bandit', 'Oarsman' F1 hybrid or 'Porbella'.

It is claimed that rust is worse on nitrogen-rich soils and suggested that an application of sulphate of potash will help to reduce its damage. Apply in early summer at 35g per sq m (1¼oz per sq yd). Always remove all infected material and burn it. Use a long rotation period, allow more space between each leek and plant only on well-drained soil. If rust is a regular problem, grow your leeks in containers. It may also occur on onions.

Harvesting

Start lifting the early varieties in early autumn. Push in a garden fork by the side of the leek you wish to lift and lever the prongs downwards, thus lifting the leek out of the soil. You can leave your leeks in the ground right through the winter, especially if they are the winter-hardy types, and harvest as needed.

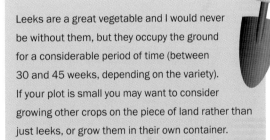

Leeks are a great vegetable and I would never be without them, but they occupy the ground for a considerable period of time (between 30 and 45 weeks, depending on the variety). If your plot is small you may want to consider growing other crops on the piece of land rather than just leeks, or grow them in their own container.

Remember, if you do not want to earth up your leeks because you do not have the time, or you are growing them in containers, you can grow them without earthing them up. Plant them as I have recommended on page 90 (dropping them into a hole) and just let them grow naturally. You will not produce quite as long a white shank as you would if you earth them up, but the stems will be a reasonable size.

If you have some leeks remaining in the ground in late spring and you want to start preparing your seedbeds, simply lift the leeks with as much soil as possible and replant them close together in a spare patch of ground and use them as necessary.

Christine's tips

Garlic

Garlic is widely used for culinary and medicinal purposes. It is generally raised from single cloves.

Growing your crop

As with any overwintered crop, a good well-drained soil is important. The soil should be reasonably fertile, having had manure added to it for a previous crop.

Break down the garlic bulbs to split them into individual cloves. During mid- or late autumn plant the individual cloves 4cm (1½in) deep so that the tip is just below the surface (like onions and shallots: see page 85). Plant the cloves 10cm (4in) apart in the row and leave 15–20cm (6–8in) between each row. Make sure you plant them the right way up, with the larger flat end (the basal plate) facing downwards.

Hoe the soil regularly to keep the crop as weed free as possible to prevent competition for light and nutrients.

Particular problems to watch out for

Garlic suffers the same problems as bulb onions (see page 85).

Harvesting and storage

Once the leaves start to turn yellow the garlic should be lifted, normally from late summer to early autumn. Do not leave them in the soil too long or the bulbs split and start to regrow. The best way to store garlic is in a well-ventilated, frost-free shed in the same way as for onions.

'Solent White'   'Purple Moldovan'

Which variety should I grow?

Both autumn- and spring-planting varieties are available. I have never been successful with this crop when I have planted it in the spring so I now always plant in the autumn.

'Iberian Wight' – plant in the autumn or spring

'Picardy Wight' – has a pink hue to the cloves; plant in the spring

'Purple Moldovan' – plant in the autumn

'Solent White' – good keeping qualities; suitable for either autumn or spring planting

Plant *bulbs*	February
	October–November
Harvest	July–September

Don't try to grow garlic if you have very heavy or badly drained soil.

Handle garlic carefully as it bruises easily and this may lead to rotting when stored.

Christine's tips

chapter 8

BRASSICAS

What is a brassica? This is the name given to any plant which is a member of the *Brassicaceae* (*Cruciferae*) family. Strictly this includes such vegetables as horseradish, mustard, swedes, turnips and watercress, but it is generally reserved for members of the cabbage family. They are cultivated either for their green leaves, for example cabbage; for their axillary buds (see page 100), for example Brussels sprouts; or for their immature flowerhead, in the case of cauliflower.

BRASSICAS When growing brassicas in an ornamental garden, ornamental cabbages are usually used. It should be remembered that other members of this family are not the most decorative and in my opinion are best planted in the vegetable garden rather than in flower beds. They can, however, be grown very successfully in containers.

You will need to consider the length of time you are happy for your ground to be occupied, as most brassicas will be in the soil for between 20 and 45 weeks. This may not be the most productive way to utilise a small piece of land. If you are keen to grow brassicas in a small space look at the seed catalogues for patio or mini varieties as these are fine for containers and small gardens. Suitable varieties are mentioned for each crop where relevant. All brassicas require moisture-retentive, well-manured soil to succeed.

Cabbages

By careful planning and choice of variety you can have cabbage maturing throughout the year. The seasons – spring, summer or winter – in the descriptions of varieties refer to the harvest date and not the planting date.

Sowing your crop

Sow from early spring to early summer for summer, autumn and winter cutting and in late summer for spring-heading cabbage. Prepare the seedbed (see page 49) and take out a drill 2cm (¾in) deep and sow your seeds very thinly along its length. You can leave the seedlings to grow on where they are, if sown in their final positions, or transplant from the seedbed later.

'April'   'Durham Early'

'Greyhound'   'Celtic' F1

'January King'   'Redcap' F1

Which variety should I grow?

'April', 'Durham Early' – spring cabbage
'Candissa', 'Greyhound' – summer cabbage
'Celtic' F1, 'January King' – winter cabbage
'Redcap' F1, 'Shelta' F1 hybrid – mini or patio
varieties; summer cabbage

Spring cabbage	
Sow *direct*	mid-July–August
Harvest	April–May
Summer cabbage	
Sow *direct*	March–June
Harvest	August–September
Winter cabbage	
Sow *direct*	April–May
Harvest	October–February

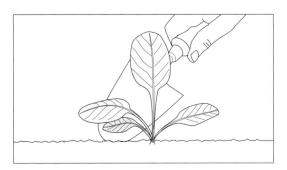

Plant brassicas deeply with the stems buried

Growing your crop

To prepare your plot for planting, fork over the soil lightly, then use a rake to level the ground before firming it.

Once the seedlings have germinated and are about 6cm (2½in) tall, thin the plants to leave them about 10cm (4in) apart. Once they have produced three true leaves, they are ready for transplanting to their final growing positions.

Water the row a few hours before lifting the plants and then finally space the crop depending on the size of head required (see Christine's tip). Plant deeply by positioning the bottom leaves of the plant at soil level, fill in the hole with soil and firm really well to help to produce cabbages with compact, tight heads.

Hoe the soil regularly to reduce competition from weeds. Keep a look out for caterpillars and other pests and take action if needed. During the autumn, winter and spring check to see if any of the plants have been loosened by frost or wind; if they have, re-firm them.

To extend the season of spring cabbage, cut off the head when it is ready to harvest but leave the stem in the ground. Next cut a cross in the top of the stump to encourage secondary growth from the cut stems. You can harvest this growth when the leaves are 10–15cm (4–6in) long and use them as spring greens.

Growing cabbages in containers is possible but aim for a minimum soil depth of 30cm (12in). The mini or patio varieties are best for this situation and remember very firm planting is required.

Particular problems to watch out for

Variability is very common among many ordinary varieties of the brassica group, so if you require all your plants to be vigorous and even in growth choose an F₁ hybrid.

Apart from factors inherent in the seed, certain cultivation techniques may lead to *variation in crop development*. Loose planting, over-application of fertiliser, very high levels of organic matter, sandy soils and pricking over the bed before planting can all lead to variability. One way of overcoming this is to firm the plant in extremely well when planting. As a test for whether you have planted it firmly enough, you should not be able to pull the plant out of the soil without breaking it.

Many brassicas grow quite large and often suffer from being blown by the wind. This is known as *wind rock* and can be prevented by deep planting at planting time. Always plant brassicas with the bottom leaves touching the soil and firm in very well.

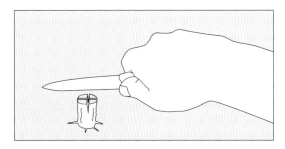

After harvesting spring cabbages, cut a cross on the stumps

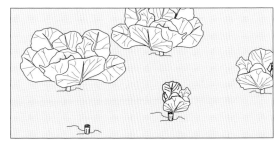

The cabbages will regrow as spring greens

Both the foliage and the roots show symptoms of clubroot

Clubroot causes poor growth, discoloured leaves and wilting in warm weather. When the plants are removed from the ground the roots are swollen, with reduced root hairs. Do not compost the plants, but lift any that have come under attack and destroy them. Ensuring the pH is above 7.5 will reduce the incidence, as will only growing the crop on well-drained soils and practising good crop rotation. Overcome the problem by growing resistant varieties such as 'Kilaton' F$_1$ hybrid.

Several species of butterfly and moth are attracted to brassicas. These are the small cabbage white, the large cabbage white and the cabbage moth and they will all produce *caterpillars* which will eat holes in the leaves of all brassicas. The main period of damage is between mid-spring and mid-autumn.

Regular daily inspections of the underside of the leaf will often reveal the eggs, which should be crushed. Prevent damage by growing the crops under horticultural fleece. Apply an insecticide when damage is first seen, paying particular attention to the underside of the leaves.

The symptoms of *cabbage root fly* include poor growth, blue-tinged leaves and wilt in warm weather. When you lift the plants, all the fine root hairs will have been eaten and frequently small white maggots are seen near or on the roots. Cabbages will fail to form hearts (and cauliflowers will produce very small heads).

Prevent the problem by putting 15cm (6in) discs of carpet or carpet underlay, roofing felt or purchased discs around the stems of the plant at planting. These stop the fly from laying eggs at the base of the plant. Draping fine horticultural fleece over the crop will also prevent damage, but ensure the edges of the fleece are well secured in the soil.

Harvesting and storage

You can cut most cabbages as required and use them immediately or store in a cool, dry room for up to seven days. Spring cabbage can be harvested and then the stumps used to produce spring greens (see opposite).

Remember that plant spacing influences the eventual size of the crop. By experimenting with the spacing in the row and between the rows you will find different-sized crops can be achieved. For example, with summer cabbage, spacing the crop 35 x 35cm (14 x 14in) will give small cabbages which are suitable for most families, while at 45 x 45cm (18 x 18in) much larger heads will be produced along with slightly earlier hearting. Winter types may be sown 45 x 45cm (18 x 18in) apart.

Christine's tip

Brussels sprouts

Brussels sprouts are grown for the buds which develop in the axils of the leaves (axillary buds). By careful planning and the use of different varieties it is possible to harvest sprouts from autumn to early spring.

Sowing your crop

Prepare the seedbed (see page 49), take out a drill 2cm (¾in) deep and sow the seeds thinly. Once the seedlings are about 8cm (3in) tall, thin them out to 8cm (3in) apart.

Growing your crop

Plant out into their permanent growing position once three true leaves have been produced. F1 hybrids may be spaced 70–80cm (28–32in) between the rows and the plants. Ordinary varieties may be spaced 60cm (24in) apart each way. Plant deeply, as described for cabbages (see page 98), and ensure they are well firmed in. Then grow on as for cabbages. As they start to gain height, stake them individually.

When growing sprouts in containers I have found it better to grow them in deep, wide pots so that when they are staked there is enough soil to support the stake securely and to prevent the pots or containers from being blown over. Use shorter varieties, such as 'Franklin' F1 and 'Early Half Tall'.

Particular problems to watch out for

All brassicas suffer the same problems (see page 98).

Harvesting and storage

As the sprouts mature the lower leaves turn yellow. Remove these to help increase the air circulation, which in turn helps to reduce the risk of disease.

With ordinary varieties, start to pick from the bottom of the stem and move upwards as the sprouts mature. F1 hybrids tend to mature all at once and should be picked and eaten or frozen. Do not store sprouts that have been attacked by pests and diseases.

Which variety should I grow?

Two different types of sprout can be grown depending on your requirements. The F1 hybrids are often compact in growth and produce a large amount of even-sized sprouts all along the stem which mature at the same time. The ordinary or open-pollinated (see page 171) varieties produce their sprouts maturing from the bottom of the stem upwards. The sprouts of the latter will sometimes blow open and lack the uniformity of the F1 hybrids.

F1 hybrids

'Revenge' – maturing from early to late winter
'Trafalgar' – maturing from early winter to early spring
'Maximus' F1 – produces buttons over a very long period from September to February, depending on sowing date

Ordinary varieties

'Bedford Winter' – matures mid-autumn to late winter
'Evesham Special' – matures early autumn to early winter

'Revenge'

'Trafalgar'

'Maximus' F1

'Bedford Winter'

Sow *direct*	March–June
Harvest	September–February

Once the plants are 30cm (12in) tall I always stake them as I generally find that, at some stage in the autumn or winter, winds will blow the plants over or possibly dislodge them in the soil, which results in loose sprouts being produced.

When all the sprouts have been picked the growing point (the green growth at the top of the plant) may be harvested and cooked like spring greens.

Christine's tips

Cauliflowers

Cauliflowers are grown for their collection of undeveloped flower buds which form the curd. By careful choice of varieties, and with the right soil conditions, it is possible to harvest cauliflowers in almost every month of the year.

However, it is often suggested that they are not the first crop a novice should try and you may require a bit of experience before you are successful with them. They should not receive a check to growth or they tend to produce small or deformed curds, so if possible sow the crop where it is intended to mature.

This crop occupies the soil for a long time, anything between 20 and 50 weeks. If space is limited it may be better to grow faster-maturing crops to make more use of your plot, or produce mini-cauliflowers (see Christine's tip).

I have never seen these plants being used in an ornamental situation and personally have never been able to produce a decent crop in containers. I have far better luck when they are planted in the garden.

Sowing your crop

For sowing times consult the packet or the catalogue. Prepare the seedbed (see page 49), make a drill 2cm (¾in) deep, and then station sow 2–3 seeds at the following spacing:

Summer cauliflowers: 45cm (18in) apart in the row and 60cm (24in) between rows.
Autumn cauliflowers: 60cm (24in) apart in the row and the same between rows.
Winter and spring cauliflowers: 70cm (27in) apart in the row and 70cm (27in) between the rows.

Growing your crop

Once the seedlings are about 10cm (4in) tall, remove the two weakest plants and re-firm the remaining plant and water well. Grow on as for cabbages (see page 98). However, to ensure they do not receive a check to growth in dry weather water, if possible, at a rate of 22 litres per sq m (4¾ gallons per sq yd) every two weeks.

When the cauliflowers start to form, bend a few of the outer leaves inwards to protect the curds from sun in the summer and frost in the winter.

Particular problems to watch out for

All brassicas suffer the same problems (see page 98).

Harvesting and storage

Cut your curds when they are a good size but while they are still tight and not showing any gaps between the florets. You can store cauliflowers for 7–10 days by pulling up the whole plant and hanging it upside down in a cool, well-ventilated shed.

Cauliflowers freeze well. Freeze only those that are undamaged and free from pests and diseases.

Which variety should I grow?

'Snowball'

'Autumn Giant', 'Snow Prince' F1 – summer and autumn
'Snowball' – summer, autumn and winter
'Belot' F1, 'Concept' – autumn and winter
'Galleon', 'Patriot' – winter and spring

Summer cauliflowers	
Sow *direct*	March–April
Harvest	August–September
Autumn cauliflowers	
Sow *direct*	April–May
Harvest	September–November
Winter and spring cauliflowers	
Sow *direct*	May
Harvest	February–May

Where space is limited try growing mini-cauliflowers. At the spacing suggested below small curds about 5cm (2in) in diameter will be produced, which are excellent for small portions or for freezing.

Space sow 2–3 seeds 15cm (6in) each way in the row and between the rows. Thin when they are about 8cm (3in) tall to leave the strongest seedling. Generally the curds will be ready 14–16 weeks after sowing. They soon start to go over, so harvest the curds when 4cm (1½in) in diameter.

Suitable varieties include 'Avalanche', 'Candid Charm' F_1 and 'Sydney'.

Christine's tip

sprouting broccoli

This crop occupies the land for a very long time, up to 40 weeks, and you may prefer to use your plot for faster-growing crops to get the most out of it.

However, it does produce fresh crops from late winter to late spring when other vegetables are in very short supply, so if you have the space it may be worth trying.

Sowing your crop

Prepare the seedbed (see page 49) and sow the seeds as you would for cabbage, making a 2cm (¾in) drill. Thin out as described for cabbage (see page 98).

Growing your crop

When the seedling has produced 3–4 leaves and is about 8cm (3in) tall it is ready for lifting. Water the plants first and then replant at a spacing of 60cm (24in) in the row and the same again between the rows. Then treat as for cabbage. The plants may become top heavy, so stake if necessary. If the plants are loosened by wind or frost be sure to re-firm them.

Particular problems to watch out for

All brassicas suffer the same problems (see page 98).

Harvesting and storage

Start to pick the spears when the heads are the size of a large walnut and still closed. Snap them off, taking the central spear first and then harvest the side ones when they are about 8–10cm (3–4in) long. The best way to store your spears is by freezing.

'Claret' F1   'Early White Sprouting'

Which variety should I grow?

'Early White Sprouting' – harvest from late winter to mid-spring

'Late Purple Sprouting' – harvest from early to mid-spring

'Claret' F1 – harvest mid-spring, dark purple

Sow direct	April–May
Harvest	
Early varieties	January–March
Late varieties	March–May
Green varieties	August–October

Calabrese

Also known as green sprouting broccoli, this very underrated vegetable produces spears from early summer through to late autumn. It is a fast-growing summer vegetable, maturing 80–90 days after sowing. Pick regularly.

Sowing your crop

The sowing date will depend on the variety. Prepare the seedbed (see page 49), take out drills 2cm (¾in) deep and allow 45cm (18in) between each row. Space sow the seeds, placing three every 30cm (12in).

Once the seedlings are 8cm (3in) tall, thin to the spacing above by removing the two weakest seedlings.

Growing your crop

Water the crop regularly to aid spear formation and hoe frequently to reduce weed competition. Apply a thick mulch as this will help conserve moisture. Cultivation is the same as cauliflowers (see page 102).

Particular problems to watch out for

All brassicas suffer the same problems (see page 98).

Harvesting and storage

Harvest and store as for sprouting broccoli (see opposite).

Sow *direct*	March–June
Harvest	July–October

Which variety should I grow?

'Ironman' F1 – sow from mid-winter to early summer; harvest from early summer to late autumn

'Beaumont' F1 – sow from late winter to early summer; harvest from early summer to late autumn

'Sampson' F1 – sow from early spring to early summer; harvest from late summer to late autumn

'Green Calabrese' – sow from early to late spring; harvest from early to late autumn

'Kabuki' F1 hybrid – ideal for growing where space is limited or in containers; sow from early spring to late summer; harvest from mid-summer to early autumn

'Ironman' F1

'Sampson' F1

'Green Calabrese'

'Kabuki' F1

Try growing kohl rabi if you have failed with other brassicas. It is very resistant to clubroot, heat and drought, so you may well be successful.

It is a reasonably hardy vegetable and may be left in the ground in most parts of Britain during the winter. Store in boxes of sand if necessary.

Christine's tips

Kohl rabi

This curious member of the brassica family produces an edible swelling just above ground level. The flavour is similar to turnip but milder.

Sowing and growing your crop

For a continuous supply, sow small amounts of white- or green-skinned types from early spring to early summer and then change to the purple-skinned types.

Prepare the seedbed (see page 49), take out a drill 2cm (¾in) deep and sow three seeds every 23cm (9in), with 30cm (12in) between the rows. Grow on like cabbage, thinning to leave the plants at their final spacing (see page 98). Small thinnings may be cooked. If you want to transplant any of the seedlings, do this when they are about 5cm (2in) tall.

Particular problems to watch out for

All brassicas suffer the same problems (see page 98).

Harvesting

Fork out of the ground when the swollen part is about the size of a tennis ball, before they become woody.

Which variety should I grow?

Three different skin colours exist: 'Green Delicacy' – green skinned; 'Kolibri' F1 hybrid – purple skinned; 'White Danube' – white skinned

'White Danube'

Sow *direct*	
Green/white	March–June
Purple	June–July
Harvest	July–November

Kale

'Black Tuscany'   'Dwarf Green Curled'

Which variety should I grow?

'Cavolo de Nero' – kale; rich green narrow leaves
'Reflex' – curly kale; harvest for most of the year from successional sowing
'Black Tuscany' – 'black' kale
'Dwarf Green Curled' – suitable for a container or where space is at a premium

Sow *direct*	May–July
Harvest	November–April

Kale or curly kale is a valuable vegetable which is extremely hardy and reliable. It can be harvested from late autumn to mid-spring. It is also useful as an ornamental plant for the winter.

Sowing and growing your crop

Prepare the land and sow your seeds as you would for cabbage in a drill 2cm (¾in) deep. Thin as for cabbage, leaving the plants spaced 45 x 45cm (18 x 18in) apart each way. Grow in the same way as cabbage (see page 98).

Particular problems to watch out for

All brassicas suffer the same problems (see page 98).

Harvesting

Remove the young leaves and shoots from the plant, leaving sufficient foliage to produce further growth.

Grow the variety 'Black Tuscany' both in the vegetable garden and the flower garden. Its architectural shape will add interest to your flower beds in the winter.

Christine's tip

chapter 9

ROOT CROPS

What are root crops? The term 'root crops' is used to describe vegetables from more than one plant family which produce storage organs derived from stem or root tissue at or below ground level. Despite their diverse characteristics, root vegetables are often grouped together in a rotation.

A good soil structure is essential for the production of good, uniform, unblemished roots and any obstructions to root growth such as stones, chemical or compaction pans (see page 171) or organic matter which has yet to break down may cause roots to be deformed.

Experimental evidence has shown that the belief that organic material causes misshapen roots is unfounded, provided that the organic matter is well rotted and thoroughly incorporated into the soil before you grow your crops.

Carrots

By careful selection of varieties it is possible to have fresh carrots available throughout the year. Carrots grow best on sandy or peaty soils, so if your soil tends to be heavy incorporate plenty of well-rotted organic matter to help improve its structure. If you are growing carrots on heavy or stony soils or in containers, select a shorter- or stump-rooted variety such as 'Early Scarlet Horn', 'Paris Market Baron' or 'Parmex'.

Sowing and growing your crop

Prepare your seedbed (see page 49) and take out a drill 2cm (¾in) deep. Rows should be 30cm (12in) apart. Sow the seeds along the drill and cover with soil. The seeds should be sown as thinly as possible to reduce the need for thinning. This prevents soil disturbance around those plants which will remain in the soil to make full growth.

Eventually thin out the crop to leave the carrots 10cm (4in) apart. Water the drill before thinning and also after, as this will settle the soil around the roots and reduce the likelihood of carrot root fly attack (see below). If the thinnings are large enough, use them in salads or just eat them raw to enjoy their flavour.

Hoe through the rows to reduce weed competition and to help conserve water (for details on when and how much to water, see page 64). Keep an eye on your crops for pests and diseases and take action if necessary. The major pest of carrots is carrot root fly.

Particular problems to watch out for

Carrot root fly will not only attack carrots but also parsnips. Leaves sometimes go reddish

Carrot root fly

and wilt in warm weather and later in the season may go yellow. The roots are disfigured by tunnelling creamy white maggots, leaving a rusty brown line on the surface of the root. There are no chemicals with approval for the amateur gardener so prevention is the best course of action.

Cover the rows or containers with horticultural fleece, or delay sowing the maincrop until early summer as this will miss the first generation of the pest. It is also a good idea to use a resistant variety (see below). Water the crop both before and after thinning but do not leave thinnings on the soil surface.

'Early Nantes'   'Chantenay'

Which variety should I grow?

'Early Market', 'Early Nantes', 'Ideal', 'Mignon', 'Paris Market Baron', 'Parmex' – suitable for containers
'Flyaway' F₁, 'Maestro' F₁, 'Resistafly' F₁ – carrot root fly resistant

Cropping times
'Early Nantes', 'Parmex' – earliest
'Nigel' F₁, 'Supreme Chantenay Red Cored' – summer
'Carson', 'Honeysnack' – autumn
'Carson', 'Red Intermediate' – winter

Sow *direct*	April–June
Harvest	July–October

Harvesting and storage

Pull carrots as they are needed. Some will normally be ready for pulling 10–12 weeks after sowing. Lift autumn and winter varieties for winter storage in mid-autumn. Remove all the soil from the roots and cut off the leaves to within about 2cm (1in) of the stalks on the top of the carrot. Store them in a box or dustbin of sand. Do not allow the carrots to touch each other: leave a small gap between each one. This helps prevent diseases or pests spreading. Store only those roots which are free from blemishes caused by pests and diseases.

It's often suggested that you grow a carrot root fly-resistant variety alongside a non-resistant variety. This allows carrot root fly to attack the non-resistant variety which you discard while resistant varieties will be clear of root fly. But in my experience, when growing in a container just use a resistant variety by itself.

I believe that the best flavour is retained if the carrots are left in the ground. This can only be done on soils which are well drained, light and not affected by carrot root fly. If you are going to use this method, cover the carrots in mid-autumn with straw or soil. If you use soil, put some slug pellets around the top of the carrots as this will help prevent damage.

Christine's tips

Raising root crops in containers

Root crops are generally sown in the position where they will grow until harvest. This is to prevent damage to the tap root. However, if you wish to use root crops in the ornamental garden or in containers such as hanging baskets, window boxes and planters with other plants, the plants should be raised in small containers or modules first and then planted into the container.

Just sow 2–3 seeds in a small pot or module and cover with 2cm (¾in) of compost. Once germinated, grow the seedlings on. You can choose either to leave the seedlings together, where they will grow but produce small roots, or thin the two weakest ones and leave the strongest to grow on, once planted into the container of your choice.

Stump-rooted carrots (see page 112) and beetroot can look fantastic when mixed with other ornamentals in a container. Either crop can make a lovely ornamental edging to a flower border and can then be harvested at the end of the season. The fern-like foliage of carrots is particularly attractive among other plants and flowers.

If you are just growing carrots in the container then they can be sown directly into it. Do this by sowing the seeds thinly all over the surface of the pot and cover with 2cm (¾in) of compost. Thin them out as they grow, leaving 5cm (2in) between each plant.

Radishes

Radishes are members of the *Brassicaceae* (*Cruciferae*) and are grown mainly as a summer salad vegetable. You can grow radishes easily on a wide range of soil types and in containers but rapid growth is essential for tender roots to be produced. To ensure continuity, make sowings at fortnightly intervals from early spring.

Sowing your crop

Although it is normal to sow radishes in a drill 1–2cm (½–¾in) deep spaced 2.5cm (1in) in the row, with rows 15cm (6in) apart, you can also sow them in the following way. Just sow the seeds thinly on the surface and then rake them into the surface lightly. This method is known as broadcasting and it is ideal for crops which require little or no thinning. Thin out as necessary as the roots start to develop, allowing 2.5cm (1in) around each root.

As a marker for slow-germinating crops such as parsnips, if you sow the radishes and parsnips together the radishes will germinate first showing you where the parsnips are before they germinate. Remove the radishes as they grow. To grow radishes as an intercrop, see page 31.

Sow summer crops fortnightly from early spring through to late summer. Thin the crops as the roots start to develop. Keep a close eye on the crop, as once they start to develop they do so very quickly and can become woody if not harvested regularly.

When not direct sowing into a container, raise the plants by sowing two seeds in small pots or modules and once 2.5cm (1in) tall move them into the container of your choice, allowing 2.5cm (1in) between each plant.

Growing your crop

When grown in rows, hoe regularly to reduce weed competition. Water the plants frequently in dry weather to encourage rapid growth. Protect against birds by placing fleece or netting over the rows.

Particular problems to watch out for

Flea beetle is a pest which may attack radishes, making tiny holes in the leaves (see page 118).

Flea beetle

Harvesting

Pull the radishes when they are about the size of your thumb.

Which variety should I grow?

'French Breakfast'

'French Breakfast' – fast-growing radish which is great to use if children want to have a try at seed sowing, as results can be obtained in six weeks

'Rainbow Mixed'

'Rainbow Mixed' – a selection of different-coloured radishes with golden skinned, purple, white and red; great for adding interest to a salad

'Rougette'

'Rougette' – bright red, round roots; suitable for growing in containers, window boxes and hanging baskets

Sow *direct*	March–August
Harvest	May–October

Parsnips

Parsnips are cultivated in the same way as carrots. They tend to be very slow to germinate, especially if sown too early into wet, cold soil. It is best to wait until mid- to late spring when soil conditions are more conducive to germination. This means that the plants get away quicker and grow better.

Sowing and growing your crop

Prepare your seedbed (see page 49) and take out a drill 2cm (¾in) deep. Rows should be 30cm (12in) apart. Because parsnips produce long tap roots, it is better to station sow (see page 55) the seeds in groups of three. Once germinated, thin out to one plant per station. For small roots, and when growing in containers, space sow every 8cm (3in) along the drill, and for larger roots every 15cm (6in) along its length.

Hoe the soil regularly to reduce competition from weeds. Water as detailed on page 64 and keep an eye open for pests and diseases.

Particular problems to watch out for

The major problem to watch out for is *canker* and the best way to get round this is to use a resistant variety (see panel).

Parsnips may come under attack by *carrot root fly* (see page 112).

Harvesting and storage

Start to harvest your parsnips once the leaves die down. This is normally in the latter half of autumn. Use a fork to lift them and shake off all surplus soil. The flavour usually improves after the first frost, so be patient and wait if you can. Lift the roots as you want them and leave the rest in the soil, but cover them with straw or soil as for carrots (see page 113).

'Avonresister'   'Gladiator' F1

Which variety should I grow?

'Dagger' F1, 'White Gem' – suitable for containers
'Avonresister', 'Gladiator' F1, 'Panache', 'Tender and True' – canker resistant
'Gladiator' F1 – good beginner's variety

Sow *direct*	late March–May
Harvest	November–March

Parsnip seed deteriorates very quickly when stored in an unsealed container in a heated room, so be sure to store them correctly (see page 46).

Christine's tip

Turnips & swedes

Both turnips and swedes belong to the brassica family and should, if possible, be on the same rotational section as other brassicas. Both are sown in the same manner. Swedes generally take about 24 weeks to mature, whereas turnips mature in half that time and are normally grown from successive sowings made from early spring onwards. Swedes are grown from a single sowing made in late spring.

Sowing and growing your crop

Prepare your seedbed (see page 49) and take out drills 2cm (¾in) deep and 38cm (15in) apart. Sow your seeds very thinly. Cover the drills with soil and water if dry.

As soon as the seedlings are large enough to handle, thin them in stages until they are 15cm (6in) apart for your early turnips or when growing in containers or where space is limited, 30cm (12in) apart for your maincrop turnips and 23cm (9in) apart for your swedes. Hoe the soil regularly to reduce weed competition and water as described on page 64. Keep an eye open for pests and treat them if necessary. The major pest of these crops is flea beetle (see below).

Particular problems to watch out for

To avoid the problem of *foliage mildew* on swedes, sow in mid-spring in colder regions and in late spring or early summer in milder, warmer areas.

Flea beetle may be a problem on brassicas, turnips and swedes. Occurring early in the season, any time from mid-spring small holes appear in the leaf but no pest can be seen. Growth is slowed and a severe attack can kill seedlings. The problem is worst in dry weather. Hoeing between the rows is said to help. Prevent the problem in the first place by covering the crop with horticultural fleece.

Harvesting and storage

Early turnips are generally not stored but are best used as soon as possible after lifting. They should be the size of a golf ball. You can lift maincrop turnips in mid-autumn and store them in the same way as for carrots (see page 113). Swedes are generally left in the soil until needed because of their hardiness.

'Snowball'   'Marian'

Which variety should I grow?

Turnips

'Aramis', 'Primera' F1 – suitable for containers or where space is limited
'Golden Ball', 'Market Express' F1, 'Snowball'

Swedes

'Invitation', 'Marian' – resistant to clubroot and mildew. 'Ruby' – resistant to mildew

Turnips	
Sow *direct*	March–May
Harvest	July–December
Swedes	
Sow *direct*	May–June
Harvest	October–March

Turnips may also be grown from an early autumn sowing for their tops, which can be cut and used like spring greens. Cut the leaves when 10–15cm (4–6in) high.

Christine's tip

Beetroot

Beetroot should be grown in soil that contains plenty of organic matter to help prevent the soil from drying out during summer. Incorporate a generous amount of well-rotted compost when preparing the seedbed.

Each beetroot seed is in fact a capsule containing two or three seeds, making thinning necessary. However, plant breeders have now bred capsules containing single seeds and these are known as monogerm varieties. These varieties require less thinning.

Which variety should I grow?

'Boltardy'

'Chioggia Pink'

Four different colours are now available:

'Burpee's Golden' – yellow

'Cylindrical' – golden/yellow

'Boltardy', 'Kestral' F1 – red

'Chioggia Pink' – pink

'Detroit White' – white

'Solo' F1, 'Moneta' – monogerm varieties

'Baby Beet Action', 'Pablo' F1 – suitable for containers or where space is limited

'Burpee's Golden'

Sow *direct*	March–July
Harvest	June–October

Sowing and growing your crop

The seed of beetroot is quite large thus making it possible to station sow your crop (see page 55), which reduces the job of thinning the plants later.

Prepare your seedbed (see page 49) and make a drill 2cm (¾in) deep. The rows should be 18cm (7in) apart for early-maturing crops, with two seeds sown every 10cm (4in). Sow only one seed if using a monogerm variety. For the maincrop and the maximum yield of medium-sized roots, have the drills 30cm (12in) apart and sow two seeds every 2.5cm (1in). Cover with soil and water if necessary.

Once the seeds have germinated, thin the seedlings and leave the strongest plant to grow at each station. Hoe the soil regularly to keep weed competition to a minimum. Apply 5cm (2in) of mulch if possible, to help conserve moisture, and water as explained on page 64.

Direct sow if growing in containers, putting one seed 2cm (¾in) deep every 10cm (4in) in each direction. Once germinated, thin to leave one seedling per station.

Particular problems to watch out for

Bolting can be a problem. The crop may run to seed before forming a decent-sized root. This may be caused by sowing the seed too early in the season, leaving the crop too long before harvesting it, allowing it to become too dry for too long or growing it in soil that is short of organic matter. Grow a resistant variety such as 'Boltardy'.

Harvesting and storage

Pull small beetroot as required but lift the maincrop in mid-autumn, being careful not to damage any roots. Use a fork to lift the beetroot, shake off all the surplus soil and then twist off the foliage, leaving about 5cm (2in) of the stalks in place. Store as for carrots (see page 113), keeping only undamaged roots.

On well-drained soils in mild areas you can leave the roots in the soil through the winter. Twist off the foliage and just cover them with straw or soil.

Potatoes

Potatoes belong to the *Solanaceae* family, along with tomatoes, aubergines and peppers. They are grouped according to the minimum time from planting to lifting. This varies from 100 days for the earlies to 120 days for the second earlies and 140 days for the maincrop, depending on the weather.

Is it worth growing potatoes on my small vegetable plot?

Generally, unless you have a lot of land I would not suggest growing maincrop potatoes as they take up too much room which could be used for the production of quicker-yielding crops.

Maincrop potatoes are also reasonably cheap to buy, so you might as well try to get the maximum economic return from your land. However, for their taste and for the savings that can be made, I think it is worthwhile growing some earlies even in a small garden or in a container.

When should I buy and plant my 'seed' potatoes?

Buy your virus-free 'seed' potatoes from mid-winter, but do not plant them until they have begun to sprout. As soon as you have obtained your tubers put them upright side by side in eggboxes or something similar, placing the ends with the most dormant eyes at the top. Leave them like this in good light (but not brilliant sun) for about six weeks, during which time several shoots will have formed. The potatoes are ready for planting when the shoots are about 2.5cm (1in) long.

This process is known as chitting.

Planting your crop

Planting should take place depending on the soil conditions and prevalence of frost. Normally earlies can be planted in mid-spring.

The simplest method is to prepare the seedbed (see page 49), then put down a garden line and use a trowel to plant a tuber 15cm (6in) deep every 30cm (12in) along the row. Leave 40cm (16in) between each row. Be careful not to break any of the shoots when planting the tubers.

Once the crop comes through the soil the shoots will need protection from frost. Do this by covering them with soil. This technique is known as earthing up, and will need to be done several times until the sides of the mounds are about 25cm (10in) high. Before the first earthing-up session takes place, sprinkle 140g per sq m (5oz per sq yd) of a general fertiliser such as Growmore along the rows; water as described on page 64.

'Accent'   'Swift'

Which variety should I grow?

Any of the following are great for boiling and serving with butter for that 'new' potato flavour:
'Accent', 'Arran Pilot', 'Foremost', 'Maris Barb', 'Pentland Javelin', 'Rocket', 'Swift'

Plant *tubers*	March–April
Harvest	June–August

Growing early potatoes in containers

Whatever container is used, it should be at least 30cm (12in) deep, with drainage holes (see page 32). Fill the container with 15cm (6in) of good quality soil or compost and place two chitted potatoes 10cm (4in) apart. Cover the tubers with 10cm (4in) of soil or compost and water well. Place the container in a light but sheltered spot and make a note of the date on which you planted it up.

Once the shoots are 15cm (6in) tall, put another 10cm (4in) of soil or compost in the container. Continue doing this until the leaves are 5cm (2in) from the top of the container. Keep the plants moist by giving them a good soaking every 10 days in dry weather.

Particular problems to watch out for

Potato blight is not normally a problem with the early crop, but remove all foliage at the end of harvesting and do not leave it lying about. Either compost it or destroy it.

Harvesting

When the flowers start to wither, lift your earlies by placing a fork just to the side of the mound of soil, pushing it in and shaking it as you lift it to reveal the tubers. Do this both for those growing in the ground and in containers. For those varieties that are flower shy or may not produce flowers, allow 100–110 days before knocking the plants out of the pots or containers.

When earthing up, do not make the side too steep or the new tubers will grow through the surface and become green and inedible.

Christine's tip

chapter 10

SALAD LEAVES

SALAD LEAVES The range and variety of crops now used for salad is exciting and flavoursome. Quick to grow and productive, they are ideal for the beginner and more experienced gardener alike. Most can be grown in very little soil, making them perfect for windowsill gardening and containers, and they are a great crop to start children off due to the speed of growth and rapid results. Because of their variety of leaf shape, colour and habit of growth, they are good for use in the ornamental garden, as edging plants or among flowers, and even in window boxes or hanging baskets.

Nearly all of them cannot be stored for more than a few days and only if a fridge is available. To enjoy them at their best eat as soon after harvest as possible.

Lettuce

Lettuce is usually grown for the leaves which, depending on the type being grown, may be tightly packed as in the cos, butterhead and crisp types, or loose as in the loose-leaf types and the cut-and-come-again salad leaf varieties which are now very popular.

By careful planning and the use of protection it is possible to produce lettuce all year round. Make sowings every 14–20 days to ensure continuity.

Lettuce has a very short shelf life once cut, and will stand in the ground for only a short time (7–14 days) when mature. This period is very much reduced in hot, dry conditions. It must grow rapidly and it is essential that the soil is light yet moisture-retentive. If your soil is well drained, incorporate lots of well-rotted organic matter to help conserve moisture.

Lettuce may be raised in several ways. It may be sown either direct in drills or sown and transplanted from the seedbed, or it may be raised in a container (see chapter 4 for details of these methods).

One of the easiest methods with salad leaves, I find, is just to fill a seedtray or shallow container with a minimum depth of 4cm (1½in) to within 6mm (¼in) of the top, level this and firm gently, and then sprinkle seeds very thinly over the surface. This method can also be used in a shallow window box or in a hanging basket. Sieve a light covering of soil over the seeds and water using a fine rose spray.

Place the tray on a kitchen windowsill from late winter or on a patio from late spring onwards. Within 7–10 days young seedlings will be through the surface and within 4–6 weeks you can start picking the leaves. Do not remove the whole plant as these will grow on to produce up to four or five more pickings. This is known as cut-and-come-again growing. Starting a new tray off every 15–20 days will ensure you have a continuous supply.

Sowing your crop in the ground

Start by preparing the ground and then take out a drill 12mm (½in) deep (see page 52). Rows should be 23cm (9in) apart for mini-lettuce and 30–35cm (12–14in) apart for other types. Normally, unless you require a large amount of salad leaves, one row is generally enough. Sow the seeds thinly, cover with soil and water well.

Summer/autumn lettuce	
Sow *under cover*	March
Sow *direct*	late March–July
Harvest	June–October
Early winter lettuce	
Sow *direct*	August
Harvest	October–December
Mid-winter lettuce	
Sow *direct*	September
Harvest	January–March
Spring lettuce	
Sow *direct*	August–September
Harvest	April–May

Which variety should I grow?

There are so many varieties these days that the choice is vast. Many are very beautiful, with varying shades of green and red leaves available and different shapes, making them ideal for growing in the flower garden as well as in the vegetable plot.

Cos types
'Claremont' – upright heads of dark green leaves
'Freckles' – spotted leaves making it suitable for both the vegetable garden and for growing among flowers

Butterhead types
'Cassandra' – pale green leaves which are resistant to downy mildew and lettuce mosaic virus; great for growing outdoors throughout the year
'All the Year Round' – very hardy; dry weather tolerant; producing medium-sized heads

Crisp types
'Black Seeded Simpson' – may be grown and harvested as a baby leaf or left to produce large crispy hearts

Iceberg type
'Match' – an Iceberg type; tolerant of hot weather; resistant to mildew; slow to bolt

Loose-leaf types
'Frillice' – much crisper than most loose-leaf varieties
'Salad Bowl' – a mix of red and green curled leaves

Salad leaves
(suitable for cut-and-come-again)
'Baby Leaf Salad' mix – a blend of leaf lettuce which is ready in just a few weeks; depending on the source it may also contain spinach, rocket, mizuna or red mustard; the different leaf shapes and types make it very effective when grown with flowers
'Lollo Rossa' – this red-leaved variety is highly decorative and adds a bit of colour to the salad; it also makes a good edge to the flower border

Where space is limited or when growing in containers, window boxes or hanging baskets:

'Baby Leaf Salad' mix (see Salad leaves, left)
'Little Gem' – compact heads
'Mini Green Improved' – produces a lettuce suitable for one person, a crisp mini-Iceberg type
'Tom Thumb' – little butterhead

'Claremont'

'Freckles'

'All the Year Round'

'Black Seeded Simpson'

'Frillice'

'Baby Leaf Salad'

'Lollo Rossa'

'Little Gem'

Growing your crop

Once the seedlings have germinated and are easy to handle, water the row and thin them: mini-lettuce 15cm (6in) apart, butterheads 25cm (10in) apart and all other types 35cm (14in) apart. If you lift the surplus seedlings carefully they can be used to plant up further rows.

Slugs can be a problem so take action to prevent damage. Keep the plants well watered (as detailed on page 63) and look out for signs of pests and diseases. Hoe the soil regularly to reduce weed competition.

Particular problems to watch out for

Greenfly (aphid) is a small sap-sucking insect which may cause puckering and distortion, along with a sticky honeydew deposit. Greenfly may also carry mosaic virus. Attacks are worse in dry weather. Spray with an insecticide when damage is first seen.

Mosaic virus may cause veins that are almost transparent to appear. The leaves become mottled and yellow or pale green in colour, with a mosaic pattern. Often the whole plant is stunted. Prevent the problem by using good quality seed and treating greenfly when first seen. Grow a resistant variety such as 'Cassandra', 'Claremont' or 'Corsair'. Good hygiene and crop rotation will also help.

Downy mildew produces yellow patches on the surface of the leaves while white mould develops underneath. Later, brown patches appear, causing the leaves to die. This disease is a problem in wet conditions. Avoid growing plants too close together. Prevent it occurring by using a resistant variety such as 'Chartwell', 'Match' or 'Multy'.

Slugs and snails feed on the leaves, leaving holes, rough edges and slime. Prevent damage by using slug pellets, or create a physical barrier (see page 168).

Harvesting

Cut individual plants once they are at a size that is suitable for your use. Salad leaves and cut-and-come-again types may be harvested when the leaves are 5–8cm (2–3in) high.

Greenfly

Mosaic virus

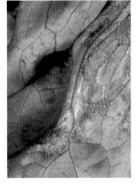
Downy mildew

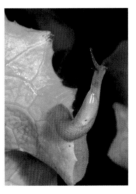
Slug

Cos lettuce form tighter hearts if they are tied together. You can do this easily with an elastic band when the plants are about 15cm (6in) tall.

Christine's tip

Grow endive as a cut-and-come-again vegetable (see page 126), in which case harvest the young leaves about six weeks after sowing.

Christine's tip

Endive

This popular salad vegetable is being more widely grown these days by salad fans for its slightly bitter lettuce taste. The crop is quick to grow with heads being ready in 10–12 weeks. Endive will tolerate light frost so is useful into the autumn.

Sowing and growing your crop

Do not sow this crop too early as it may bolt. Ideally sow from early spring to early autumn.

Prepare the seedbed (see page 49), take out a drill 1cm (½in) deep and then sow the seeds thinly along the rows, which should be 30cm (12in) apart. Cover with soil and water well. Once the seedlings are about 5cm (2in) tall, thin the crop to leave plants 23cm (9in) apart in the rows. Successive sowings will ensure a continuity of supply.

Particular problems to watch out for

All salad and leafy vegetables suffer the same problems (see page 128).

Harvesting

The crop is normally ready for harvesting about 10–12 weeks after sowing.

Which variety should I grow?

'Pancalieri' – a frizzy leaf type which produces rose-tinted white mid-ribs; self-blanching; bolt resistant

'Pancalieri'

Sow *direct*	April–August
Harvest	September–February

Corn salad

Which variety should I grow?

'Cavallo' – small leaves with a neat habit of growth

'Cavallo'

Sow *under cover*	February–March
Sow *direct*	March–August
Harvest	April–October

Corn salad (Lamb's lettuce) produces its crop of salad leaves in the autumn and winter when lettuce crops have gone over. This leafy vegetable can be grown as a come-and-cut-again crop (see page 126) and is a useful plant for intercropping (see page 31).

Sowing and growing your crop

Prepare the seedbed (see page 49) and take out a drill 1cm (½in) deep with rows 15cm (6in) apart. Sow the seeds thinly, cover with soil and water well. Once the seedlings are about 5cm (2in) tall, thin them so they are 10cm (4in) apart in the row and use the thinnings in your salads.

Particular problems to watch out for

All salad and leafy vegetables suffer the same problems (see page 128).

Harvesting

Pick only a few leaves at a time so as not to defoliate the plant, normally 4–12 weeks after sowing.

Celery

In small gardens I do not think it is really worth growing the traditional trench grown crop as it takes up a lot of space. A much easier option, providing you can keep the crop well watered, is the self-blanching type.

Sowing and growing your crop

This crop is not easy to start into growth by sowing outside, so I grow it on a kitchen windowsill or in a greenhouse until it is ready to be planted out. Seed is slow to germinate.

Sow the seeds in pots or seedtrays containing a seed and cutting compost. Do not cover the seeds with compost as they need light to germinate. Place in a temperature of 15°C (59°F). Once the seedlings have produced one true leaf prick them out into either modules or small pots. Keep growing on until

Which variety should I grow?

'Galaxy'

'Galaxy' (Lathom Self-Blanching) – can be sown early without running to seed; produces crunchy, tender stems

'Loretta' F1 – vigorous variety producing smooth, crisp, white sticks

Sow *under cover*	March–April
Plant *out*	May–June
Harvest	September–February

the plants have between four and six true leaves before hardening off and then planting out into the garden. If planting out during cold weather, protect the crop for the first 2–4 weeks with horticultural fleece, removing it when the weather is warmer.

Space the plants about 25cm (10in) apart in a block and water well. Ensure that the crop is kept well watered otherwise the sticks will be stringy. Apply 22 litres per sq m (4¾ gallons per sq yd) once or twice a week during dry spells. Mulching the crop will help conserve moisture.

Particular problems to watch out for

All salad and leafy vegetables suffer the same problems (see page 128).

Harvesting

Lift as required. The crop should be ready about 25 weeks after sowing. Take from the outside of the block first, using a trowel, so that you do not disturb the plants remaining in the soil.

spinach

Spinach has a very distinctive flavour and may be eaten raw or cooked. It is now a very popular addition to salads and mixed salad leaves. Keep the crop well watered in dry spells otherwise the leaves may become tough.

Sowing and growing your crop

Prepare the seedbed as described on page 49. If you are going to grow spinach as a come-and-cut-again crop, incorporate a balanced fertiliser such as Growmore at a rate of 35g per sq m (1¼oz per sq yd). Take out a drill 2cm (¾in) deep with rows 30cm (12in) apart. Sow the seeds thinly, cover the drill with soil and water well. Once germinated, harvest as a salad crop when the leaves are small. If growing the plants on to maturity, thin the crop in the rows to 15cm (6in) apart.

Particular problems to watch out for

All salad and leafy vegetables suffer the same problems (see page 128).

Harvesting

Harvest leaves when about 8–10cm (3–4in) long as a salad crop. If growing on to maturity, the crop normally takes 10–12 weeks to mature. Remove leaves from mature plants as required.

'Bordeaux' F1   'Medania'

Which variety should I grow?

The following varieties can be sown from early spring:

'Bordeaux' F1 – produces lovely red stems and veins against a dark green leaf; great for salad leaves or steaming

'Giant Winter' – produces large, dark green leaves of excellent taste; very hardy and stands for a long time; sow between late summer and early autumn for spring harvesting

'Medania' – probably the easiest variety to grow; produces a lot of dark green leaves which stand well without bolting; may be sown in the spring and summer

'Reddy' F1 – produces attractive red stems with leaves that are ideal for use as baby salad leaves

Sow *direct*	March–September
Harvest	May–April

If growing the crop as salad leaves, pick regularly when young and tender. If growing to maturity, sever the whole plant about 2.5cm (1in) above the ground and leave it to re-sprout.

Christine's tip

chapter 11

CUCURBITS

Courgettes and marrows, pumpkins and squash,
and outdoor cucumbers

CUCURBITS Cucurbits are grown mainly for their edible fruits, which are harvested at various stages of maturity. Cucurbits require moisture-retentive but well-drained soil, so ensure that you incorporate plenty of well-rotted compost or manure into the soil at planting.

In the past, the older varieties which were grown were far too large for even medium-sized gardens, but nowadays smaller varieties are available, ensuring that those of us who enjoy these crops can do so in little gardens, raised beds and containers. I often see these smaller varieties being grown up balcony rails or balustrades.

All can be grown in containers, but ensure nothing smaller than a 9 litre (2 gallon) bucket is used so that sufficient water may be given. I personally have not been successful growing any of these crops in grow bags.

Courgettes & marrows

I have found that one or two plants per person are ample unless you have a particular fancy to one of the crops. If you grow more you will have a glut and may end up throwing some of the crop away.

Bush-type courgettes and marrows are suitable for small gardens as they are compact and productive, most growing to about 1m (3ft) wide and up to 30–45cm (12–18in) tall. If space is limited, do not grow trailing types as these will take up far too much room.

Christine's tips

All cucurbits	
Sow *under cover*	March–April
Plant *out*	late May–June
Sow *direct*	late May–June
Harvest	July–October

'Venus' F1

'Badger Cross' F1 hybrid

Which variety should I grow?

Courgettes

'Black Forest' F1 – a climbing plant suitable for containers and for training up trellis, strong bamboo canes or strong netting. 'Defender' F1 hybrid – resistant to cucumber mosaic virus. 'Midnight' F1 – a very compact plant suitable for containers. 'Venus' F1 – grow where space is limited as it is a compact grower. 'Yolanda' F1 hybrid – resistant to cucumber mosaic virus

Marrows

'Badger Cross' F1 hybrid – bush variety (see tip), resistant to cucumber mosaic virus
'Bush Baby' – bush variety (see tip)
'Tiger Cross' F1 hybrid – resistant to cucumber mosaic virus

Pumpkins & squash

'Baby Bear'

'Festival'

Outdoor cucumbers

'Byblos' F1 hybrid

'Green Fingers' F1

Which variety should I grow?

Pumpkins

'Wee B Little' – suitable for smaller households as each fruit weighs no more than 1kg (2¼lb)

'Baby Bear' – fruits can be harvested when they weigh about 1.5kg (3¼lb)

Squash

'Festival' – a trailing variety that can be grown up supports to save space; fruits are grapefruit sized when mature

Which variety should I grow?

Outdoor cucumbers

'Byblos' F1 hybrid – resistant to cucumber mosaic virus

'Green Fingers' F1 – can be grown up a support to save space; the small-sized fruit, 10–12cm (4–5in), is a great addition to a child's lunchbox

'Sindy' F1 hybrid – resistant to cucumber mosaic virus

Sowing your crop

If you only need one or two plants it may be easier for you just to buy ones ready for planting out.

However, if you do wish to grow your own plants, sow individual seeds in mid-spring in 8cm (3in) pots of seed compost, sowing the seeds 2.5cm (1in) deep. The seed should be sown on its edge to help prevent rotting. Keep the temperature at about 15°C (59°F). Sowing the seeds individually helps the plants to develop rapidly because none of the roots are damaged when it comes to planting out.

You can sow the seeds directly outdoors once the soil temperature has risen above 13°C (55°F), which is usually in late spring. If you do sow outdoors, sow three seeds per site and thin to leave the strongest seedling after germination.

Growing your crop

Prepare a planting hole by removing the soil to a depth of 30cm (12in) and then mix plenty of well-rotted manure or compost into the soil taken out of the hole. Replace the soil mix, making a mound with the surplus soil. Spacing between the holes depends on the crop:

'Summer Ball' F1 is a dual-purpose variety of squash. It is a compact plant whose fruits can be harvested as a courgette or left to mature into a 1kg (2¼lb) pumpkin. It is ideal for growing in containers.

Christine's tip

Courgettes: 90 x 90cm (35 x 35in)

Marrows (bush types): 90 x 90cm (35 x 35in)

Outdoor cucumbers: grown on the ground 90 x 90cm (35 x 35in); up canes 45 x 45cm (18in)

Pumpkins: 1.5 x 1.5m (5 x 5ft)

Squash: 1 x 1m (3 x 3ft)

Do not plant out cucurbits until they have been hardened off (see page 56) and all risk of frost has passed (usually towards the end of spring).

Plant one plant per hole and water well. To ensure fruit is produced the plants must never suffer from drought, so in dry periods water them thoroughly twice a week.

Training

Bush varieties of courgettes, marrows, pumpkins and squash do not require any training.

If you wish to save space, grow cucumbers, pumpkins and squash up a tripod of canes or on wires stretched along a fence. As the growth is produced, just tie this in to the cane or wire.

Water around the plants, not over them, so that the likelihood of disease occurring is kept to a minimum.

Christine's tip

Pollination

Cucurbits produce separate male and female flowers and, unlike greenhouse cucumbers, the outdoor crops require pollination so it is important not to remove any of the flowers. The proportion of male to female flowers may vary during the season. Normally pollination will take place naturally by visiting insects, but if the weather is cold few insects will be active and you may well find carrying out pollination yourself to be beneficial.

This is a simple operation to carry out (see below). First remove a male flower (the one with no bulge behind the flower) and then push it inside the female flower (the one with a bulge behind it). Do this to each female flower.

 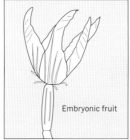

Embryonic fruit

Male flower   Female flower

Encourage visiting insects by growing sweet peas and herbs in or around the vegetable garden. If growing in containers, include pots of herbs or sweet peas with the pots of vegetables.

Christine's tip

Cucumber mosaic virus   Powdery mildew

Particular problems to watch out for

Cucumber mosaic virus is a serious disease which is spread by greenfly, so as soon as this pest is seen spray with an insecticide suitable for edible crops. Symptoms are mottled yellow and dark green patches on the leaves with distortion and puckering. Prevent the problem by growing resistant varieties.

Powdery mildew affects the whole plant and covers it in white powdery patches. There is a tendency for this disease to occur in the autumn. Grow a resistant variety and spray if necessary with a fungicide suitable for edible crops.

Harvesting and storage

All of these crops develop very quickly indeed once they start to fruit, so regular inspection will ensure the fruits do not get too large before they are removed.

Continual harvesting has a beneficial effect on these plants and encourages more fruit to be produced. Even if you do not want the fruits yourself, you can always give them away or compost them rather than leaving them on the plant, as this tends to slow down further production of the crop.

Courgettes: cut when 10–15cm (4–6in) long.
Marrows: cut when 20–30cm (8–12in) long; store in nets in a cool, frost-free shed or room.
Outdoor cucumbers: cut once the fruits are 15–20cm (6–8in) long, depending on the variety used (see the seed packet for specific details).
Pumpkins and squash: harvest before the first frost and store like marrows.

chapter 12

FRUITING VEGETABLES

Aubergines, capsicums and tomatoes

FRUITING VEGETABLES These are the crops where we harvest the fruit but think of them as vegetables, in use and cooking. Now widely available in many different shapes, sizes and colours, they add much to our plates.

Capsicums include all the different types of pepper such as sweet peppers and chilli peppers. Aubergines are often known as eggplants because these subtropical plants produce egg-shaped fruit.

Tomatoes, capsicums and aubergines all belong to the same family (*Solanaceae*) and may be grown outdoors in milder areas; otherwise they are normally grown under protection.

Aubergines

Capsicums

Tomatoes

Which variety should I grow?

Since you will only need a few plants, especially if space is limited, obtain these from a garden centre. Most of the varieties sold at such an outlet will be reliable and productive, so just read the labels and select those which appeal. It also means that you do not need the equipment and heat required to raise these crops early in the season.

Sow *under cover*	March–April
Plant *out*	late May–June
Harvest	
Aubergines	July–October
Capsicums	August–October
Tomatoes	August–October

Growing your crop

In practice I have found that, at the most, two plants of each crop will provide enough for one person and you may have a surplus if you grow more. All three

plants require a warm, sunny, sheltered position and well-drained soil.

At planting time work 125g per sq m (4½oz per sq yd) of a general balanced fertiliser such as Growmore into the soil. No more fertiliser or feeding will be needed unless you are growing them in containers. It is important to establish sturdy plants but excess feeding with nitrogen in the early stages of growth tends to produce lots of leaves at the expense of fruit, so use only a balanced fertiliser obtained from a garden centre.

Do not plant out the crops until all risk of frost has passed, probably in late spring. Plant in rows 1m (3ft) apart, with plants 35cm (14in) apart in the rows. This makes management of your plants relatively easy.

Container growing

All three crops can be grown very successfully in pots, containers, raised beds or in grow bags. I only plant two plants per grow bag. Fill the container with good quality potting compost and make sure it is no smaller than 30cm (12in) as this allows sufficient water to be given. I plant one plant per pot. Growing the plants up against a wall will give a bit more protection and heat.

When growing the plants in containers, liquid feeding should take place once the first flowers are produced, following the manufacturer's instructions. All three crops may be fed with a tomato fertiliser.

Aubergines and peppers do not need staking but upright growing tomatoes will need an individual stake.

Types of tomato

Three different types are now widely grown, which allows the crop to be grown in many different situations.

Hanging basket and container varieties (also known as determinate types) are small-growing bush types which do not need stopping or pinching. You just plant them and allow their natural habit to develop. They are great for pots no smaller than 20cm (8in), for window boxes, raised beds, hanging baskets, or even for planting in your flower border.

If planting among flowers, allow 45cm (18in) of space to give the plants room to develop their natural spreading habit. They may of course be planted into the vegetable garden if you do not fancy the taller varieties (cordon types) that need supporting, stopping and sideshooting.

Cordon varieties (also known as indeterminate types) will grow upright as a vertical cordon and will need to be tied to an individual stake. Once growing they should be tied to the cane every 20–30cm (8–12in). Sideshoots will start to grow in the leaf joints and these should be removed as soon as possible. If left to develop they sap the strength of the plant, resulting in low yields.

Once the plants have produced 4–5 trusses (bunches) of flowers, remove the growing point of the plant. This encourages the fruit to develop and ripen.

Hanging basket and container varieties

Sideshooting a tomato

Dwarf varieties

Cordon varieties

Dwarf varieties will only grow to about 20cm (8in) tall and require no stopping or pinching. They are great for growing on a windowsill, in window boxes, in hanging baskets or in 15cm (6in) pots. They are very attractive as an edging in the flower garden and are great plants for children to start growing their own.

Particular problems to watch out for

Generally the main difficulty with growing these three crops is poor weather. If it's a dull or damp year you may well struggle to produce a decent crop. The main problem that you may experience is tomato/potato blight.

Tomatoes can suffer from *potato blight*. This disease normally appears from mid-summer and is worst in a damp, humid season. The symptoms are brown edges to the

Potato blight

leaves, brownish black patches on the fruit and the stems of the plant and collapse of the plants. Although fungicides do exist, in my experience you are better removing the plants and burning them to prevent further problems. Try growing blight-resistant varieties such as 'Legend' or 'Ferline' F1.

Harvesting

Once the tomatoes start changing colour and are ripening, pick individual fruits. Sweet peppers may be harvested once the fruits are glossy and a usable size. Delaying harvesting and allowing the fruits to become large will reduce the amount of crop produced.

Coloured fruits (reds and yellows) may take up to six weeks to change colour. To ensure a long cropping season, chilli peppers should be harvested while the fruits are still immature.

Aubergines are ready for picking when the fruit is smooth, with a glossy skin and of a reasonable size. This is normally towards the autumn.

chapter **13**

HERBS

and edible flowers

HERBS Growing herbs in and around the vegetable garden is an excellent idea. It provides you with a supply of fresh herbs which are always better than those that have been dried, they look great and complement the vegetable garden, and they will attract beneficial insects, which in turn will help with pollination and pest reduction.

In a small garden I think they are best grown along the edges of the paths. In this way you do not have to go on to the plot when the weather is wet to pick a fresh supply. This not only keeps your feet clean but prevents you causing compaction to the soil when it's wet.

Germination of some herbs can be slow and often for the frost-tender plants, such as basil, you need to sow them with heat under protection to get good results. Garden centres have such a wide range of herbs these days that, if you only need one or two plants, obtain them from such a supplier. Buying the plants eliminates the need for a propagator or a greenhouse and overcomes some of the difficulties in raising these popular plants.

Herbs do best in a warm, sheltered, sunny situation and well-drained soil, and they all appreciate some space, so do not plant them too close together.

Rosemary can make a great hedge around the vegetable garden, as can *lavender*. On a windy site it may give enough protection to allow you to start your vegetables off a couple of weeks earlier in the season than you could otherwise.

Mints can be invasive and the runners they produce will spread if they are not restricted. This can be achieved by planting them in a container. Remember to put drainage holes in the container if it has not got any already. *Lemon balm* may also spread quickly and to restrict its growth, just as you can do with mint, plant it in a container.

Basil is frost tender and suffers badly if planted out too soon. Wait until early summer when all danger of frost has passed and it should establish and grow well.

Growing your crop

Many herbs benefit from having their growth cut back in the early summer as this encourages busy growth and the production of new fresh leaves. Reducing the plant by a third of its size will keep the plants in check and growing neatly.

When I first started to grow herbs I did not appreciate the difference between annual herbs and those which are perennial. I often mixed them up when planting. After the first year I was disappointed to find that several had died and did not come back into growth. These, I found out later, were the annual ones. The following is a list of common herbs which are annuals: basil, chervil, coriander, dill, pot

marigold, purslane and savory. These may die at the end of the year, depending on the weather. However, some may survive if the winter is mild enough. If they do need replanting, obtain the new plants from a garden centre.

If you would like to grow a few herbs on your windowsill, herb seed mats are available from some seed companies. These are mats containing seeds which are placed on the surface of plant pots filled with compost and then watered. The plants are just grown on in the same pots.

Growing herbs in containers, window boxes or hanging baskets, or on a patio, balcony or courtyard is very rewarding. Ensure that all the containers have drainage holes and use good quality soil-based potting compost such as John Innes. I prefer soil-based compost as it is heavier and helps prevent pots being blown over and I believe herbs live longer in soil-based compost.

A 45cm (18in) hanging basket that gave me a great deal of pleasure and fresh herbs was planted up with thyme, rocket and oregano in the bottom of the basket, with basil, chives, mint and summer savory in the top. I have seen French marigolds planted with parsley looking great together.

If you grow thyme over the edge of a window box there will be room within the box to plant lemon balm, oregano, rosemary and sage.

EDIBLE FLOWERS These can add a lot to desserts, baking, drinks, salads, soups, sauces and ice cream. Their use has been documented since Roman times and nowadays they are frequently included in recipes from Chinese, Middle Eastern and Indian cultures. Edible flowers became very popular in Britain during the Victorian era.

The main thing to realise is that you do not need a lot of flowers to give a dish flavour or colour, so use with care. It should also be mentioned that some may aggravate particular allergies or intestinal problems. Be careful until you know you can tolerate them.

Very much like herbs, it is unlikely that you will need more than one or two of these plants to provide you with enough for use in the kitchen. Obtain young plants from the garden centre and plant them around the edges of your flower garden. Along with herbs, they will encourage beneficial insects into the garden.

It is important to identify the flowers correctly in the first place. Do not eat them unless you are certain of their edibility. If you are unsure, either ask a gardening friend or consult a good reference book. Not all flowers are edible and it is generally only the petals rather than the whole flower head that are used in cuisine.

Pick the flowers when it is cool, either in the morning or evening, as this will help prevent them wilting. Shake every flower to remove any insects or dust hidden within and then place them in a bowl of salted water for half an hour. Remove carefully and allow them to dry on kitchen paper, but do not place them in a sunny position as this may make them wilt quickly.

If you wish to store a few flowers overnight you can do this by putting the whole flower into a glass of water in the fridge. Keeping the flowers cool and dark will ensure they stay in good condition.

Only use flowers which have not been sprayed with garden chemicals. Those obtained from nurseries, garden centres and florists may have been sprayed with a pesticide. Very few of these outlets will stock organically grown flowers. Also remember that any flower picked from near a road may have been sprayed, so again I would not recommend this practice.

Courgette flowers   Runner bean flowers

Edible vegetable flowers

Alliums include leeks, chives, garlic and shallots. Their flowers, which have a stronger flavour than the leaves, can be use in soups and salads.

Arugula, also called garden rocket, produces leaves which are used as a baby salad but the small, white flowers with a dark centre and a piquant flavour may also be used in a salad.

Artichoke is mainly grown for its crown but the leaves of the flower are also eaten.

Broccoli forms an edible green head which is actually the flower buds. When these are allowed to open they are yellow and have a mild broccoli taste and are excellent for use in stir-fries and salads.

Courgette, **marrow** and **pumpkin** flowers may be dipped in batter, shallow- or deep-fried and eaten.

Pea flowers are the garden pea, NOT the ornamental sweet pea, which is poisonous. The white flowers have a slightly sweet taste similar to peas. The shoots and tendrils may also be eaten.

Radish flowers, depending on the variety, may be pink, white or yellow and have a flavour similar to the root. These flowers may be added to salads.

Runner beans have lovely red flowers which are delicious in soups and salads or served as a garnish.

Edible flowers

Calendula (also called pot marigold) (*Calendula officinalis*) gives us petals which are spicy and similar in taste to pepper. Use in salads and rice and pasta dishes. The petals will add a yellow tint to soups and scrambled eggs.

Chicory (*Cichorium intybus*) petals have a bitter taste and are often used as a garnish.

Cornflowers (*Centaurea cyanus*) are commonly used as a garnish but the petals have a clove-like taste. Used commonly as a natural food dye.

Dandelion (*Taraxacum officinalis*) flowers should be picked when young. They have a honey-like taste and may be used in salads or sprinkled over rice just before serving.

Day lilies (*Hemerocallis* spp.) are a great addition to salads for their sweet melon taste. Some people say the different-coloured flowers taste differently but I can't say I've noticed.

Dill (*Anethum graveolens*) flowers may be used in soups for their tangy flavour.

Fennel (*Foeniculum vulgare*) produces yellow flowers which have an anise taste that is good in desserts, soups or as a garnish.

Fuchsia (*Fuchsia* x hybrids) flowers come in a vast range of colours and shapes which makes them great for use as a garnish. They have a slightly acidic taste.

Calendula   Chicory

Gladiolus (*Gladiolus* spp.) flowers taste a bit like lettuce but may be used as a dish for sweets or mousses. The petals may be used in salads.

Hibiscus (*Hibiscus rosa-sinensis*) flowers have a citrus flavour and may be added to salads or used as a garnish.

Impatiens (*Impatiens walleriana*) flowers taste sweet and may be used as a garnish or floated in drinks.

Lemon verbena (*Aloysia triphylla*) has tiny, cream- coloured flowers that give custards and flans a citrus flavour.

Mint (*Mentha* spp.) flowers taste very much like the leaves and may be used in the same manner, for example in drinks or salads and for flavouring.

Nasturtiums (*Tropaeolum majus*) are my favourite. They have a taste very similar to watercress and may be used in salads.

Pansies (*Viola* x *wittrockiana*) have a grass-like taste and make soups, salads and desserts interesting.

Roses (*Rosa rugosa* or *R. gallica officinalis*) petals taste similar to strawberries. They can be added to ice cubes and used in drinks; they may be sprinkled on to salads or used in jellies and ice creams.

Savory (*Satureja hortensis*) flowers have a hot and peppery taste similar to thyme. They are good for using in soups.

Scented geraniums (*Pelargonium* spp.) have flowers that generally taste like the plant. Hence citrus-scented flowers have that tangy, peppermint-like taste. They may be used in salads, desserts and in drinks.

Thyme (*Thymus* spp.) flowers taste very similar to the leaves and are good in soups.

Cornflowers

Day lilies

Fennel

Lemon verbena

Mint

Pansies

Rose

Savory

chapter 14

PROBLEMS

Weeds, pests and diseases

WEEDS

What is a weed?

A weed is generally defined as a plant growing where it is not wanted. For example, a potato in a carrot bed is a weed and a thistle among peas is a weed. But it does not have to be a plant that normally grows in the wild of the countryside which then seeds and grows in among your vegetables. It can be any plant where you do not want it. Weeds may do any of the following:

~ harbour pests and diseases
~ cast shade
~ compete for water, plant nutrients, light and space
~ make lifting or harvesting a crop difficult

They are grouped depending on their life cycle, and fall into two types: annuals or perennials. This knowledge is used in controlling them, to gain maximum effect from the different methods used.

Annual weeds

An annual is a plant which germinates, grows, flowers, sets seed and dies in one year. Some, however, may complete the cycle several times in one year, only taking a few weeks to go round the entire life cycle. These are known as ephemerals and examples are groundsel (*Senecio vulgaris*) and chickweed (*Stellaria media*). This increases the number of seeds that are produced and hence the amount of weeding that you will have to do.

Some seeds can remain dormant for many years, while others only have a short life. If you cultivate your garden regularly, generally between 45 and 50 per cent of the weed seed that are produced each year are lost through exposure to the weather, eaten by birds or germinate too deeply in the soil and die before they reach the surface. A few are destroyed by pests and diseases or are eaten by mice.

Regular weeding will help lower this figure by reducing the number of seeds set. Try not to let your weeds flower and set seed because some plants, such

as fat hen (*Chenopodium album*), can produce up to 70,000 seeds per plant in one life cycle. There is a saying in the world of gardening that goes 'One year's seeds, seven years' weeds'. So try to prevent the problem in the first place.

Competition from weeds has the most damaging effect on plants three weeks after germination: you must remove the weeds while they are still small. Concentrate on the weeds between the rows as these are more competitive than those within the row of plants and so cause more damage.

The most practical method of control for annual weeds is to hoe or weed by hand. If the weather is warm and dry, small weeds hoed off or pulled up may be left on the surface to wither and shrivel up, but if the conditions are damp they may re-root when left on the surface. I personally just weed straight into a bucket, which can be tipped on to the compost heap, providing the weeds are not in flower or diseased.

Perennial weeds

A perennial is a plant which grows for more than two years, and perennial weeds are often the ones which cause the gardener the most problems. They include couch grass, docks, ground elder, horsetail, rosebay willow herb and thistles.

Many perennial weeds are deep-rooted or have underground storage organs which enable them to survive in cold winters. Being deep-rooted also means they grow well under drought conditions, whilst your crop plants suffer.

Most perennial weeds produce fewer flowers than annuals because they spread by vegetative means. If you just hoe perennial weeds off in the summer they will often sprout again from their roots. Learn to recognise them and, when you are digging over your plot in the winter, remove them together with all the little pieces of root or rhizome. Even small pieces of root left in the soil will cause you problems the following year.

The best way to control perennial weeds is to dig them up or use chemical weedkillers (known as herbicides).

When you are digging be as thorough as possible so that you remove all the weeds. In the long term this will save you time.

To make hoeing easier and safer in the seedbed put a small quantity of radish seed in the drills of slow-germinating crops. These will germinate quickly and allow you to see where the crop will develop and the row position. You will then be able to hoe between the rows without causing any damage.

Christine's tips

Controlling weeds

Weed control can be carried out in different ways:

~ hoeing
~ pulling the weeds by hand
~ using heat via a flame gun to kill them
~ mulching to smother them
~ using chemicals.

If time allows, you can also use cultural methods (see page 164).

Hoeing This is one of the most effective methods of removing weeds. There are three types of hoe available and it is important to select one which you feel comfortable using.

~ *Onion hoe* Use a chopping action, drawing the blade towards you while walking forward so that you can see what you are doing. Avoid walking on your plants!

~ *Draw hoe* Use as above. The hoe is long-handled, so you do not have to bend as much as with the onion hoe.

~ *Dutch hoe* Use by moving the blade back and forth, parallel to the surface of the soil, entering the soil very shallowly so that you cut off the roots of the weeds just below the surface. With this hoe you walk backwards, hoeing the soil that has been trampled on.

Keep the blade of your hoe clean and sharp. This will make the job much easier and will cut the weeds more efficiently too.

Do not hoe too deeply or the seeds of other weeds will be raised to the surface. Deep hoeing will also bring damp soil to the surface, resulting in the loss of more soil moisture than is necessary.

Hoe in dry sunny weather, so that the weeds soon dry out and wither.

Hand pulling This is a slow method of weeding, and is generally used only if the weeds have become quite large. You walk through your plants, pulling out individual weeds. These are best removed before they flower or set seed, and at this stage they may be composted. Otherwise, burn them. Do not leave weeds to become too large or they may be difficult to remove.

Using a flame gun This tool produces a flame, which you pass over the weeds to scorch them. A few days later, when the weeds have withered, you go over the area again and completely burn off the remaining growth. You do need to be careful between close-spaced crops, but I find this an excellent method of weed control.

Mulching With this method, you cover the soil surface with a layer of organic material, resulting in the soil below the mulch being kept moist during dry spells if an adequate layer of 8cm (3in) is applied. The mulch will smother annual weeds and those that do germinate are easily removed. Depending on the material used, the mulch may release plant nutrients and improve the soil structure over a period of time (see page 36).

Materials that are commonly used for mulching in the vegetable garden include well-rotted compost, paper, cardboard, leaf mould, mushroom compost and grass clippings (these should be composted first).

Mulching helps conserve water and reduces weed growth

Chemical weed control There are only a few weedkillers that are suitable for the vegetable garden. I myself do not use any, but an awareness of the types available is helpful. It is also good to know that you can buy ready-to-use (RTU) weedkillers in containers, so removing the job of having to handle the concentrate or measure chemicals out, or the need for separate equipment to apply the weedkiller.

When you go into a garden centre you may be confronted by packets or bottles with labels you do not understand. The information in the following paragraphs will help you select the type of chemical you need.

~ *Contact* A contact weedkiller destroys only the plant tissue which it contacts and does not move very far within the plant. It will kill annual weeds but perennials may regrow. These weedkillers are useful for getting rid of weeds between plant rows but you must be careful to avoid contact with the growing crop. This can be done by using a watering can with a dribble bar attached.

~ *Translocated* A translocated weedkiller enters the leaves and moves to other parts of the plant. It is especially useful for controlling perennial weeds on ground where no crop plants are growing.

~ *Residual* This is a chemical that will remain active in the soil or crop for some time. It is generally used on land that is not being cropped at the time.

Cultural weed control The main form of cultural control is the use of a stale seedbed. This is a seedbed that is prepared as normal and then left untouched, to allow the weed seeds to germinate. The weeds are then hoed off or sprayed off using a contact weedkiller. The more often this process is repeated before the crop is sown the better, and timing depends on the need for use of the land. It would be great if you could leave it for a whole season.

When you finally sow your seeds, do so with the minimum of disturbance, to avoid bringing new weed seeds to the surface.

PESTS AND DISEASES

What are pests and diseases?

Crop pests are animals, mainly insects, whose action causes the malformation or destruction of crop plants, and the consequent reduction in quality and/or quantity of the crop for human consumption. They may be either parasites or predators.

Diseases in plants may be caused by fungi, bacteria or viruses, and are usually recognised by the symptoms they produce in the affected plants. They may be spread by certain pests, chiefly insects, which are known as vectors.

Some pests (slugs and snails, for example) will attack a wide range of plants, while others (such as the cabbage root fly and the carrot root fly) are highly specific and will only attack one group of plants. The recognition and treatment of specific pest and disease problems are dealt with under each crop.

However, pests and diseases should not be a major issue if plants are grown well, unless you are surrounded by others who allow problems to build up without taking evasive action.

Pest and disease damage

The effect of the pest or disease on the plant very much depends on when the damage is caused.

When seeds or seedlings have been affected by pests or diseases, the plants may not develop. If they do develop, they may be disfigured and consequently useless. Damage at this stage may be critical, and you should keep your eyes open for problems and take appropriate action as soon as you see the first signs of trouble.

As the plants grow larger, the significance of damage depends on which part of the crop is being used. For example, flea beetles will eat the foliage of radishes without much damage to the part you eat and so, if the radishes are nearly ready for harvesting, there is no need to worry. On the other hand, carrot root fly damage to carrot roots makes them unsuitable for storing – a real blow if your crop is specially

intended for winter use.

Generally the same comments apply to the fungal and bacterial diseases. Action taken depends on the nature of the damage, when it occurs and the use you wish to make of your plants. It is for you to decide how much damage is acceptable. We don't always need perfect results.

Viral diseases are more serious and should be watched closely. Most viruses are spread quickly, often by greenfly (aphids), and can result in total crop failure. As soon as you see any greenfly, control them; and if you do have any infected plants, remove them and burn them as soon as possible to prevent the problem spreading. Viral diseases themselves are incurable.

Seasonal changes in insect numbers

The weather has a major effect on insect populations. If the weather is very cold at the time of egg laying, most insects do not lay as many fertile eggs as they might and many of those laid fail to develop at low temperatures. Insect flight, too, may be restricted in cold weather, which may in turn prevent the fertilisation of eggs and thus lead to a reduction in the size of the insect population.

Other insects are adversely affected by particularly wet or dry weather. Red spider mite are very much reduced in wet weather. They need hot weather to survive, and they reproduce much more quickly if it is hot and dry rather than damp.

The presence or absence of natural enemies of the pests, such as parasites, predators and disease organisms, will also influence numbers each season.

Avoiding pest and disease damage

Once again, prevention is better than cure. I very seldom have any pests or diseases as I tend to protect those crops that I know are likely to suffer. For example, I use horticultural fleece on carrots and all the brassicas and take out the tips of broad beans before they get heavily infected with blackfly.

You can also help to avoid damage by ensuring that your soil is fertile, at the correct pH and well drained. Giving plants good growing conditions, which includes growing them at the correct spacing and with the right amount of food and water, will result in healthy, strong plants which can stand up to damage much better than weak plants.

Sowing your seeds thinly into warm, well-prepared soil will help get all your plants off to a good start and they will quickly become established and grow strongly. Do not allow your plants to become overcrowded. Thin them as soon as possible, to give ideal conditions to those left to develop.

Take the following actions to help you avoid problems:

Practise garden hygiene A clean garden looks good but also helps reduce plant health problems.

~ Most pests and disease organisms need shelter and moisture during some part of their life cycle and you are doing them a favour if you leave heaps of plant material, rubbish and old pots and boxes around your garden. A preventative measure is to clear it away.

~ Do not leave old cabbage stalks or other plants in the soil to overwinter, as these can harbour pests and diseases which may survive until the spring and cause new infestations.

~ Remove all weeds which may play host to pests and diseases.

~ Remember not to compost any plant which is infected with pests and diseases. Burn it immediately.

Always plant healthy material
~ Do not grow plants which have been given to you by a friend who you know has problems in their garden, as you could be introducing the problem into your own garden.

~ Check that plants from garden centres or nurseries are free from greenfly and that they look sturdy and healthy. If they don't, leave them on the shelf and go elsewhere for your plants.

Grow disease-resistant cultivars or varieties Plant breeders have utilised such characteristics as hairiness of the cultivar, waxiness, thickness of the surface layers, early maturity and vigour, plus other genetic features, to breed new plants which are resistant to certain problems. I have mentioned resistant cultivars and varieties under the relevant crops.

Practise crop rotation (see page 28) If practised properly, crop rotation helps to reduce certain problems in the garden, such as clubroot of cabbages.

Be aware of plant density Growing plants very close together may result in conditions conducive to pest and disease attack. Keep an eye open for problems when there is little space between plants and treat them immediately you see the symptoms.

Adjust sowing and planting dates For example, early sowings of peas will avoid damage caused by pea moth (see page 72); late sowings of carrots will help avoid the first generation of carrot root fly maggots (see page 112); and late plantings of cabbages and cauliflowers will help prevent damage caused by flea beetles (see page 118).

Protecting brassicas against cabbage root fly

Controlling pests and diseases

Regular inspection of your crops will enable you to
see any problems developing and then you can take
immediate action, using one of the methods outlined
below. I have also given further information in the
instructions for growing specific vegetables.

Physical methods There are several physical
methods you can use to control pests, but for any
method to be successful it must be carried out
consistently to ensure that no pests escape. Here are
some examples:

~ Prevent insects laying eggs by placing horticultural
fleece over rows of crops that may be affected, such as
carrots and peas.

~ Hand-pick eggs and caterpillars from brassicas.

~ Crush greenfly, which are often present in only
small numbers at the start of the season. Obviously, if
there is an infestation this would be too messy.

~ Protect brassicas against cabbage root fly damage
by placing circles of cardboard or a similar material
around the stem of the plants (see above).

~ Use physical barriers such as nets, fences and cages
to give protection against rabbits, cats and birds. This
is a simple and very effective method of control.

~ Use traps to control pests such as mice which may
attack your peas and beans. Place your trap near the
rows but not on top of them, so that the mice do not
disturb the soil.

~ Make a physical barrier of grit, eggshells, crushed-
up seaside shells or finely chopped hair to prevent
slugs and snails damaging the crops. I personally have
never found any of these methods to work but others
say they do, so I think it's worth trying them in your
own situation and seeing if they work for you.

Control diseases by removing infected leaves, flowers
or fruit, to reduce the spread of infection.

Biological control Biological pest control makes
use of a 'good' insect to kill a harmful one and has
been going on for years in nature. Ladybirds and
lacewings, for example, kill and eat greenfly.

Outdoor biological control methods are subject
to weather and temperature fluctuations. Unless you
follow the instructions to the letter, control can be
very disappointing.

What is important, however, is to maintain the
natural enemies of pests in the garden, like ladybirds
and lacewings. Encourage natural enemies into the
vegetable garden by growing nectar-rich flowers and
herbs which are attractive to them, such as golden

Biological pest control

rod, lavender, marjoram, night-scented stock, pot marigold and red valerian. Avoid killing beneficial insects through the incorrect use and application of chemicals, be they organic or synthetic.

Chemical control Recently we have seen the removal of a vast number of chemicals used for the control of pests and diseases in our gardens. Those we still have available should be used wisely, following the instructions fully.

I know that in practice most of us read how much of the chemical should be put into a litre of water, mix it up and spray it on our plants, but please read all the instructions, not just the application rate. Many will state that the mixed solution should be applied to a specific area, should not be used when crops are in flower or when bees are active, or only applied to the underside of the leaves, for example.

Remember also that the chemicals for sale are very specific in how they work. For example, an insecticide will only control insects, not a fungal problem, and a fungicide will only control a fungal infection, not a pest attack.

The instructions given on the bottle or packet are there to ensure that you get the best from the chemicals in the safest manner to you, your plants and the environment. If you bear in mind that the majority have been recommended in the past for use in commercial horticulture, you will appreciate that they do work, when used correctly.

I do use slug pellets if I have to, but follow the instructions very carefully. They are much more effective applied at the recommended spacing of 8–10cm (3–4in) than when applied by the pepper pot method of placing so many down that the ground looks blue. This is definitely a case of less is more.

Where to get advice

Good control depends on the correct identification of the problem. Once the problem has been identified you should be able to acquire the correct material to control it. I have supplied information about pests

and diseases in the instructions for growing crops, but if you are not sure what the problem is or how to control it, seek advice from a garden centre or one of the following sources:

~ Speak to a member of an allotment or horticultural society. Your local authority will be able to provide contacts.

~ Join the Royal Horticultural Society (RHS), 80 Vincent Square, London SW1P 2PE. Tel 0845 130 4646 www.rhs.org.uk

~ Join the National Society of Allotment and Leisure Gardeners (NSALG), Head Office, O'Dell House, Hunter Road, Corby, Northants NN17 5JE. Tel 01536 266576 www.nsalg.org.uk

~ Read *Grow It!*, a monthly magazine for the kitchen and vegetable grower. It contains articles giving practical advice on all aspects of producing food in anything from containers to large-scale plots. Subscription details from Kelsey Publishing Group, Freepost SEA2268, Westerham, Kent TN16 3BR. Tel 01959 541444 www.growitmag.com

Some magazines offer help with identifying problems, but when sending the sample off, avoid putting it in a plastic bag as after a short while it may well have become a foul-smelling mess. Put tissue paper or kitchen roll around the sample and place it between two pieces of card, then put inside a dry polythene bag. It will stay fresh like this for a few days. Send the sample by first-class post, avoiding weekends and bank holidays if you can.

Some agricultural and horticultural colleges offer help, but always telephone first. The Royal Horticultural Society advises its members.

Christine's tips

GLOSSARY

Acid soil: a soil which has a pH below 7 and which is therefore lacking an abundance of free lime.

Alkaline soil: a soil with a pH above 7 and which therefore has ample free lime present.

Ammonium sulphate: an inorganic fertiliser which supplies nitrogen.

Annual: a plant that germinates, grows flowers and sets seed in one growing season.

Atmospheric nitrogen: gaseous nitrogen in the soil.

Axillary bud: a bud which grows from the angle where a leaf stalk joins the stem or a smaller stem joins a larger one; for example, a Brussels sprout is an axillary bud.

Band: a strip alongside a crop where fertiliser is applied.

Base dressing: a fertiliser applied to the soil immediately before sowing or planting.

Biennial: a plant which completes its life cycle within two growing seasons.

Blossom end rot: a more or less rounded dark brown or black area of skin at the blossom end of a fruit, caused by a calcium deficiency.

Bolting: the premature flowering of the crop (sometimes described as running to seed).

Brassica: a member of the *Brassicaceae* family which used to be known as the *Cruciferae*; for example, cabbage, cauliflower, kale, sprouts, swedes and turnips.

Broadcast sowing: scattering seeds over the surface instead of in a drill.

Capping: the destruction of the soil surface, resulting in all the particles settling out into their individual sizes causing a hard crust or cap to form in dry weather.

Catch crop: a quick-maturing plant grown between the harvesting of one vegetable crop and the planting of the next on the same piece of land.

Caterpillar: the larva of a moth or butterfly.

Check: a term used to describe the point when a plant stops growing and developing. This may be as a result of many factors such as drought, very cold weather, pest and disease damage, and physical damage.

Chitting: a term used when starting a seed or tuber into growth before sowing or planting.

Compaction: the consolidation of soil particles, resulting in the restriction of air and water movement through the soil.

Compound fertiliser: a fertiliser which contains all three of the major nutrient elements (see chapter 3).

Cotyledon(s): the seed leaf (leaves), which is (are) generally the first to emerge above ground. These frequently look nothing like the adult plant's leaves.

Cucurbit: a member of the cucumber family, including courgettes, cucumbers, marrows, pumpkins and squash.

Cultivar: a distinct variant of a species, produced by plant breeding and maintained in cultivation.

Curd: the tight mass of young flower buds that make up the heads of broccoli and cauliflower.

Deficiency: a term used to describe symptoms displayed by a plant when it is short of one of the plant foods necessary for good, healthy growth.

Drill (also known as a groove): a small furrow or groove made in the soil into which the seed is sown. Depth varies according to the size of the seed. A flat-bottomed drill is one which has a flat or level base and is normally suggested for use when sowing peas or beans. The vast majority of plants are raised in a V-shaped drill or groove.

Earthing up: drawing or mounding up soil around the base of a plant.

Emergence: the process during which seed leaves (cotyledons) come above the soil surface.

Enzymes: chemicals produced in the plant which stimulate growth.

F1 hybrid: the first filial generation obtained in breeding work.

Family: a group of related genera, for example peas and beans or brassicas.

Fertilisers: substances capable of supplying plant food of which there are organic types (derived from plant or animal remains) and inorganic types (of chemical origin).

Foliage: the leaves of the plant.

Foliar feeding: a liquid fertiliser sprayed on to a plant or watered on through a watering can and directly absorbed through the leaf.

Fungicide: a chemical used specifically to kill fungi.

Fungus: a non-flowering organism which produces spores. It does not make its own food and therefore must live on another living or dead organism.

Friable: a term used to describe a fine, crumbly, workable soil.

Fruit: a fruit is derived from the ovary of the flowers which enlarges after fertilisation to accommodate the maturing seeds.

Germination: the process by which the seed absorbs water which then activates the growth enzymes, producing a root which splits the seed coat and releases the leaves and shoots. This all occurs below ground.

Growing season: the time from sowing or planting a crop to harvesting.

Growmore: a compound fertiliser containing equal parts nitrogen, phosphorus and potash.

Habit: the natural growth and development of a plant.

Hardening off: the process whereby plants raised under protection (for example, on a kitchen windowsill or in a greenhouse) are given more ventilation and lower temperatures so that they acclimatise to conditions out in the garden.

Herbicide: a chemical weedkiller.

Humus: partly decomposed organic matter.

Hybrid: a plant produced by crossing two species.

Insecticide: a chemical used specifically for killing insects.

Leaching: the washing out of soil nutrients (plant foods) caused by water draining through the soil.

Legume: a member of the pea family.

Lime: a material which is added to the soil to reduce acidity. It may contain calcium, magnesium, or both.

Liquid feeding: the application to the soil of a plant food diluted in water.

Manure: enrichment, generally organic in nature, which is applied to the soil to provide nutrients and help improve soil structure.

Marble stage: this is the size of a potato tuber normally at flowering.

Module: a form of container to hold compost; may be single or multiple units.

Mosaic: mottling of the leaves, generally caused by a virus.

Mulch: a surface layer of organic or inorganic material used to suppress weeds and conserve water.

Nipping out: see Stopping.

Nitrochalk: an inorganic source of nitrogen and phosphate.

Nutrient: plant food.

Open-pollination: this occurs where plants of the same type are growing next to each other (as in a field) and can receive pollen from any of these surrounding plants.

Organic: a substance which is derived from a source which is, or has been, living.

Pan: a layer of soil which is compacted either on the soil surface or beneath the surface.

Pelleted seeds: individual seeds coated with a clay-like material which makes handling easier.

Perennial: any plant which grows for more than two years.

Petiole: the stalk of a leaf.

pH: the degree of acidity and alkalinity, generally of the soil. Below pH 7 it is acid, above pH 7 alkaline, with pH 7 being neutral. The scale goes from 0 to 14.

Photosynthesis: the chemical process by which green plants make their own food.

Pinching: see Stopping.

Pollination: the transfer of pollen from the male flower to the female flower.

Pricking out: transferring a seedling from a seedtray or pot into another seedtray or pot, giving it more room to develop.

Resistant plant: a plant that has been specially bred so that it is not affected by a particular pest or disease.

Rhizome: a horizontal underground stem.

Sap: the liquid inside a plant which carries the food to all parts of the plant.

Seed: the mature ovule after fertilisation of the egg. It contains an embryo plant within a protective coat called the testa.

Seedling: a young plant raised from seed.

Seedsman: a company which packs seed for the retail market.

Sets: small immature bulbs used for propagation.

Shank: the white, blanched area of a leek or salad onion.

Slated soil: this occurs where the soil particles are damaged and slide to increase their size, becoming flatter than normal. When they form a sheet they may prevent seedlings emerging.

Smeared soil: this occurs where soil particles, particularly clay, are increased in size, making a polished surface which prevents water and roots from penetrating.

Solanaceae: the potato and tomato family.

Space sowing (sometimes called station sowing): seeds are sown individually or in twos or threes at the required spacing for the crop to grow undisturbed until harvesting.

Spears: the individual flower stalks of a cauliflower or broccoli.

Spit (as in digging): the full length of a spade's blade or fork's prongs.

Stopping: the complete removal of the plant's growing point.

Tap root: a single swollen root, for example, a carrot.

Thinning: the task completed to reduce the number of seedlings in a drill or seedtray to give them more room.

Tilth: the cultivated surface of the soil. A good tilth should be fine and crumbly with no clods of earth or large stones present.

Transpiration: the loss of water vapour by plants to the atmosphere.

True leaf: the new growth produced after the cotyledons, as the plant grows.

Truss: a collection of flowers, normally used to describe tomato flowers which develop into fruit.

Tuber: a swollen underground root or stem acting as a food-storage organ.

Variety: a distinct variant of a species occurring naturally in the wild. However, it is the common term used erroneously to describe most of the different individual names given to, say, cabbage; for example, cabbage 'April' or 'January King'. Botanically these are really cultivars but in gardening you will hardly ever hear a gardener talk about a cultivar. Most gardeners talk about varieties, and this is what I have called them in this book, despite the fact that technically nearly all of them are cultivars.

Viability: the period of time during which seeds remain able to germinate.

Virus: an extremely small, disease-causing organism which can duplicate itself once inside a plant. Generally recognisable by the effects produced in the infected plant.

Water in: watering around the stem of a newly planted or transplanted plant to help settle the soil around the roots and provide moisture for new root growth.

Weed: any plant growing where it is not wanted.

Wind rock: the loosening of a plant's roots by strong winds, blowing the aerial portions of the plant about.

Harvest regularly to increase production.
Christine's tip

INDEX

Acknowledgements

I would like to thank all the staff at Simon & Schuster UK for commissioning this book and helping in all the stages of production, and for their suggestions and guidance. Sincere thanks to you all.

Picture acknowledgements All images in this book were photographed by Jacqui Hurst with the exception of the following:

Alamy /allotment boy 1 120 centre, /Dave Bevan 36 top right, 80 top left; / blickwinkel 168 right, /Christopher Burrows 120 top, 120 bottom, /David Burton 29, /Nigel Cattlin 72, 76 bottom left & right, 91 top, 99 left & centre, 115 top, 128 top right, 128 bottom left, 142 top left & right, /David Cole 149 bottom, / Digitalman 168 left, /Down the Garden Path 112 top, /Tim Gainey 140 left, / John Glover 58-59, 77 centre bottom left, 149 top right, 156 top right, 158-159, 167, /Brian Hoffman 71 bottom left, /Martin Hughes-Jones 84 bottom right, 105 bottom right, 106 top right, 122 left, /Andrea Jones 36 bottom right, / Torbjorn Lagerwall 152 top, /Andy Lane 86 top, /Bryan Lewis 165, /David Page 36 bottom left, /Jonathan Plant 128 bottom right; **Dreamstime** /Ivan Korolev 157 centre bottom right; **Fotolia** /grimplet 137 right, /Kelly Marken 37 top left, /Mattéo C. O´B. 161; **GAP Photos** /Maxine Adcock 9, 89, 90 right, 93, 104 bottom right, 139, /Lee Avison 74 top, /BBC Magazines Ltd 55 left, 60, /Pernilla Bergdahl 127 top right, /Dave Bevan 110 centre top, 128 top left, /BIOS − Gilles Le Scanff & Joëlle-Caroline Mayer 116, /Richard Bloom 92 centre, /Mark Bolton 86 bottom right, /Elke Borkowski 26, 146, /Julia Boulton 77 top, 77 bottom left, 144 centre, /Lynne Brotchie 67 top, /Nicola Browne 118 left, /Jonathan Buckley 117 bottom left/Design: Sarah Raven, 127 centre top right, /Keith Burdett 160 bottom left, /Leigh Clapp 142 bottom, /Paul Debois 110 top, 121, /David Dixon 148 bottom left, /Heather Edwards 92 left, 153, /FhF Greenmedia 61, 115 centre top, 140 centre right, /Tim Gainey 20, 140 centre right, /Suzie Gibbons/ Design: Veronica Clein 24 centre, /John Glover 104 top, 114, /Michael Howes 49 left, 87,104 bottom left, 132 bottom, /Martin Hughes-Jones 74 bottom, 100 top left, 106, /Geoff Kidd 127 bottom right, /Michael King 154 bottom, /Fiona Lea 30 right, 123, /Howard Rice 31, 156 top left/Design: Joy Martin, /Friedrich Strauss 82, 141, 157 bottom right, /Graham Strong 81, 144 bottom, 147, 148 top, /Maddie Thornhill 57, /Juliette Wade 112 centre left, /Jo Whitworth 105 top, 131 bottom, 132 top, 134 left, /Rob Whitworth 117 top, 127 bottom left, /Mark Winwood 163; **The Garden Collection** Jane Sebire 160 bottom right, / Derek St Romaine 103, 133; **Garden World Images** /Nicholas Appleby 66, /Dave Bevan 79 bottom left, /Sine Chesterman 88 left, /Francoise Davis 105 bottom left, /Gilles Delacroix 96 centre right, 102, 127 centre top left, 134 centre, /A Graham 99 right, /Martin Hughes-Jones 55 right, 100 bottom left, 115 centre bottom, /MAP 80 top right, /Trevor Sims 56, 68 bottom, 77 centre top right, 100 top right, 130, 131 top; **Getty Images** /Alan Buckingham 85, /Gallo Images/ Neil Overy 36 top left, /PhotoAlto/Laurence Moulton 129; **istockphoto** 39, / Aylieff-Sansom 156 bottom left, /canismaior 157 bottom left, /cosmonaut 134 right, /flyfoor 16, /IgorSPb 155 top, /Viktor Kitaykin 157 centre top left, /Laura's Adventures 157 top left, /Mark_VB 156 bottom right, /Nancy Nehring 157 centre top right, /Tjanze 152 bottom, /Roger Whiteway 157 centre bottom left; **Francine Lawrence** 8 top, 13, 24 bottom, 162; **Marshalls Seeds** 77 centre top left, 77 bottom right, 80 bottom right, 88 right, 95, 96 top right, 96 bottom left, 105 centre right, 122 centre & right, 127 top left, 127 centre bottom left, 138 bottom left; **photolibrary.com** /Peter Anderson 42, /Garden Pix Ltd 157 top right, /Oredia/Boutet Jean-Pierre 149 top right, /Radius Images 135; **photolibrary. com/Garden Picture Library** /Maxine Adcock 37 top right, 49 right, 67 bottom, 84 top right, 112 bottom, 113 bottom, 117 bottom right, 118 right, /Matt Anker 97, /Pernilla Bergdahl 155 bottom, /Linda Burgess 154 top, /Chris Burrows 84 bottom left, /John Carey 24 top, /Brian Carter 94, /Christi Carter 73, /Kate Gadsby 151, /Michael Howes 164, /Andrea Jones 11, 63, /Geoff Kidd 113 top, / Gavin Kingcome 84 top left, 92 right, /Mayer/Le Scanff 14-15, /A S Milton 33, / Cora Niele 83, /Howard Rice 96 centre left, 112 centre right, /Rosalind Simon 108-109, /Gary K Smith 10, 54, 150, /Mark Turner 106 top left, /Juliette Wade 71 top right, /Jo Whitworth 138 top, /Francesca Yorke 160 top; **Photoshot/ Photos Horticultural** 110 centre bottom; **Science Photo Library** /Maxine Adcock 80 top right; **Sea Spring Photos/Joy Michaud** 106 bottom, 119; **www. seedsavers.org/Becky Whaley** 71 top left; **Sutton Seeds** 71 bottom right, 80 bottom left, 90 left, 96 top left, 105 centre left, 140 right; **Thompson & Morgan (UK) Ltd** 74 centre, 77 centre bottom right, 86 bottom left, 96 bottom right, 100 bottom right, 115 bottom, 127 centre bottom right, 138 bottom right; **Christine Walkden** 22 top & bottom, 25, 27 top & bottom, 30 left, 38, 73 inset, 91 bottom, 101.